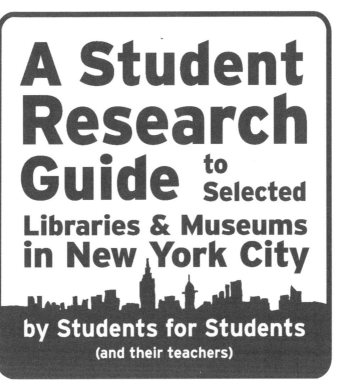

A Student Research Guide

to Selected

Libraries & Museums in New York City

by Students for Students
(and their teachers)

THE GILDER LEHRMAN

INSTITUTE *of* AMERICAN HISTORY

ISBN 0-9663843-1-8

Contents

How This Guide Came About	6
Introduction	8
American Folk Art Museum	12
American Museum of the Moving Image	16
American Museum of Natural History	18
Americas Society	22
Brooklyn Museum of Art	24
Cooper-Hewitt, National Design Museum (Smithsonian)	28
Frick Collection	32
Hamilton Grange	34
Historic Richmond Town	38
Intrepid Sea-Air-Space Museum	42
Jewish Museum	44
Lower East Side Tenement Museum	48
Metropolitan Museum of Art	50
Morris-Jumel Mansion	54
Museo del Barrio	58
Museum of American Financial History	60
Museum of Chinese in the Americas	64
Museum of the City of New York	68
Museum of Modern Art QNS	72
Museum of Television and Radio	78
National Museum of the American Indian (Smithsonian)	84
New-York Historical Society	88
New York Public Library	92
Schomburg Center for Research in Black Culture (NYPL)	94
South Street Seaport Museum	98
Statue of Liberty and Ellis Island	102
Studio Museum in Harlem	106
Whitney Museum of American Art	108
Useful Websites	110
Map	112

Notes:

How This Guide Came About

The idea for a student research guide to selected New York City museums and libraries started in 2001 as a summer project for two Gilder Lehrman Institute interns. We sent Ina Groeger, then a freshman at Columbia, and Alex de Maria, a sophomore at Vassar, to scout out some interesting places and topics that might appeal to student researchers writing history papers. What they found is in this guide. In her introduction, Ina tells you how to reach her with comments and suggestions. We'll incorporate them into the next edition, so tell us what you think.

Thanks to Richard Gilder, Lewis Lehrman, and James Basker for making the Institute's work possible, and thanks to all who worked on this guide. Howard Seretan, Education Coordinator at the Institute, thought it up and helped Ina and Alex get started. Leah Arroyo, Kathleen Barry, Peter Ekman, and Sasha Rolón edited, updated, and checked the facts. Thanks also go to the many museum educators and library staff who talked to Ina and Alex about their programs.

And special thanks to Ina and Alex, students both, who tell you what you want to know: how to get there, what it costs, and what's in it for you once you're there. And don't worry—they won't send you anywhere boring.

Lesley S. Herrmann

Lesley S. Herrmann
Executive Director
The Gilder Lehrman Institute of American History

Notes:

Introduction

The Gilder Lehrman Institute of American History is a not-for-profit organization that seeks to spread the knowledge of American history and to improve the quality of American history education. It supports scholars who write books about American history and provides free lectures by famous authors in that field.

But what makes the Institute unique is the emphasis it places on American history education at the middle and high school level. Gilder Lehrman cares about you, the student. Gilder Lehrman helps your education by enriching your teachers' knowledge of American history through special seminars and curriculum planning sessions. Gilder Lehrman funds special trips for many of you through grants to your schools. And with this guide, Gilder Lehrman gives you the information you need to explore American history in your very own back yard, one of the best back yards for exploring American history: New York City.

Who are the authors? Alex and I are college students. We started the guide two summers ago. Peter, who helped me out as I added to and updated it this past summer, is still in high school. We have all written and continue to write research papers for school, so we definitely know what they're like. And yet, while we know how much fun it is to learn (and write research papers), we also have lives outside of school. I like to knit and play field hockey. Alex loves drama. Peter is in a band and plays ice hockey.

Why write the guide? To give you an idea of great resources that are not just educational but also fun, in the many world-class institutions right here at your fingertips in New York. We were amazed by the places we visited while writing the guide, and we've tried our best to share our enthusiasm with you. So we hope that after reading through it–or at least skimming through it–you'll be motivated to visit at least one of the places we've written about for you.

Whether you just want to find a fun place that you've never been to or whether you're doing some hard-core research, this guide is the place to start.

The guide as a research tool. We don't know how many times we've considered a research topic and thought, "Where in the world am I gonna find information about this?"

Well, the best papers are ones that you are interested in writing. So we've done our best to put together information on how to study almost every area of American history that you could possibly think of. We also know that sometimes the hardest part of writing a paper is getting started, so we've tried to help you figure out not just which museums and libraries are good for which research areas, but which ones are good if you still need to find a topic.

How we wrote the guide. We went online and compiled a list of which major New York City libraries and museums seemed the most interesting and relevant for studying American history. Then we talked with people in the education department. We looked around each place and asked a ton of questions.

For each site, we wrote about current and upcoming exhibits, the accessibility of the permanent collection (if it is not all on display), research opportunities, programs for high school students and those for adults that would be helpful to you, which ones tend more toward entertainment, which ones tend to be more educational, whether you need to pay to research, and whether you need to call in advance to make a reservation.

We also tried to infuse the guide with interesting paper topics and fun facts. We should say that our guide in no way exhausts all of the museums, libraries, and research opportunities available to you, the high school student. However, it's a great source of information about where and how to learn about American history, and it's a great place to start no matter what your topic.

The museums and libraries in the guide. There is no way we could possibly include every place where students could do American history research in New York City, so we tried for a pretty good mix. We've included not just museums and libraries but also historic houses and National Park sites, exploring a range of cultures and heritages.

Just because a museum or an exhibit focuses on one area, time or culture, don't write it off. Read through the descriptions of museums and check their websites for current exhibits. You really never know what you'll find. As we made our visits, we were constantly surprised by the breadth and variety of information.

Money, money, money. Luckily, one of the things students are not expected to have much of is money. Even libraries and museums know this, so don't be put off by admission fees. Several of the fees are really suggested dona-tions, which means that you can pay whatever you want. Some places are free, and many others have at least a couple of hours a week where you can get in for free, especially if you are a student. Almost all of the places in this guide offer a discounted admission fee to students with ID.

If you really can't afford even the student fee, then call the place you want to visit and explain why you want to come, as well as the situation that prevents you from paying the fee. Museums tend not to be run by cold-hearted meanies. After all, they are there to educate you, and the last thing they want to do is to turn away students, especially those whose only reason for not visiting is their inability to pay. But you should not take advantage and ask not to pay if you can afford it. Museums and libraries require a lot of money to stay open to the public, and though the price may seem high, considering the awesome contents that you are allowed to see, it's really a token amount.

High 5. If you are a middle or high school student in New York City, you need to know about High 5. High 5 is an organization that puts aside discounted tickets to shows, concerts, and other events specifically for students. Particularly relevant to this guide is High 5's museum program. During the school week (not on the weekend), you can get two tickets for $5 at any of the participating museums. You yourself must use one of the tickets, but anyone can use the second ticket as long as they are with you. Participating museums include the American Museum of the Moving Image, the Jewish Museum, the Lower East Side Tenement Museum, MoMA QNS, the Museum of Television and Radio, the National Museum of the American Indian, the Solomon R. Guggenheim Museum, the Studio Museum in Harlem, and the Whitney Museum of American Art. For more information on High 5, check their website, www.high5tix.org/index.html.

Note to students and teachers. Many programs are geared for entire classes and take place during the school day. While some educators are willing to make the information from these programs available to individual students, they stress that it is not the same as attending the classes and encourage teachers to call to find out about the different class-oriented programs.

Note to students. We can't stress enough how amazing the resources are that we describe in this guide, and how much you really should go visit them all (or at least some of them). At the same time, we realize that these resources are scattered all over the city (can we say Staten Island?), and may require you to venture out to parts of the city you may never have been to before. While we encourage you to explore not just the sites but also the area of the city they're in, we also ask you, at the risk of sounding like a parent, to be careful. Have fun, be adventurous, but be alert. Look at a map before you go. Double-check the directions. Every place we describe can be reached by subway or bus. If you're not comfortable venturing out on your own, bring along a parent or a friend. (Remember, those High 5 tickets come in twos.)

Thank you's We would like to thank all of the museum educators and library staff who took the time out of their busy schedules to meet with us and tell us about their institutions. Their help and enthusiasm certainly made our research a lot easier and a lot more fun.

Oh, but it's not over yet, folks We want to know what you think. How helpful is the guide? How could it be more helpful? Tell us where you went and what you thought about the places you visited. Also, tell us about the places we should add to our guide. This is a work in progress that we will be adding to and updating, so we would really appreciate your feedback.

Please send all ideas, comments, and suggestions to me, Ina, at groeger@gilderlehrman.org. We will read them. And we may include students' and teachers' comments in the future. Okay, that's it. (Finally!) Enjoy the guide!

Ina Groeger

Ina Groeger
Fall 2002

Address:	45 West 53rd St. New York, NY 10019
Telephone:	212.265.1040
Directions:	Take the E, V to Fifth Ave./53rd St.
Hours:	Tuesday-Sunday 10:00am-6:00pm Fridays 10:00am-8:00pm Closed Mondays
Entry Fee:	$5 Students Fridays 6-8 Free
Website:	www.folkartmuseum.org

"Folk art? What's that?" you might think. According to Artlex's online dictionary (www.artlex.com), it's "Art made by people who have had little or no formal schooling in art." Folk artists typically use traditional techniques and content, in styles handed down through many generations, and often of a particular region. Paintings, sculptures, ceramics, metalwork, costume, tools, and everyday objects all may be folk art. **The art you'll see here personalizes American history.** Though much of it is traditional, it's less conventional and much more fun than you might expect. Almost all American, and many times religious, patriotic and/or political, the exhibits are fascinating. Definitely worth a look.

Recently the museum had on display: "American Anthem Part II: Masterworks from the Permanent Collection." Although it contained mainly American work, including several pieces by artists of color, it also had works by artists from such countries as England, Italy, India, and Switzerland. The inclusion of foreign artists into "American Anthem" reflected the museum's goal of collecting works that add more of a global perspective to the museum's exhibits.

By comparing foreign artists' work to that of Americans, you might ask yourself which, if any, themes tend to define just American folk art and which tend to permeate all forms of folk art. Pieces in the museum date from America's colonial period to the present, and the exhibit included everything from weathervanes to whirligigs, from the interior walls of a house to quilts, sculptures, toys and, not surprisingly, quite a few paintings. Where else can you see works by masters of the 20th century such as Horace Pippin, Bill Traylor, Martin Ramirez, Morris Hirshfield, Sister Gertrude Morgan, and Nellie Mae Rowe?

One exhibit you should look forward to seeing in spring of 2003 is on fraktur. Fraktur is artwork in the tradition of illuminated manuscripts: pen, ink, and watercolor drawings that accompany texts. This exhibit will focus on such work done by Pennsylvania Germans from the 1790s to the 1830s, varying from birth certificates and religious texts to teacher-made arithmetic books.

When you go to the American Museum of Folk Art, don't forget also to check out its old location, where it still has exhibits: the Eva and Morris Feld Gallery at Two Lincoln Square. Currently it's showing an exhibit entitled "Painted Saws" by Jacob Kass. If you go, you will see 60 saws meticulously painted with vignettes of bucolic landscapes and vivid cityscapes. It is definitely worth checking the website, www.folkartmuseum.org, to see what is going on at both sites. The museum and the gallery often show exhibits that complement each other.

But what kind of research topic would bring you to the museum or the gallery? A lot of topics, actually. Here are just a couple of themes to explore: Looking at the decorative furniture, you can see a Neoclassical revival in which the brand new republic looked back to the legacy of the ancient civilizations of Greece and Rome, as well as to the British, for decorative styles. In the quilts, mostly those on the 5th floor, you can see patterns with themes of patriotism and religion. Quilts and painted scenes bear religious phrases and imagery. **"American Anthem II" shows the evolution of the American identity, including certain motifs such as the eagle, the shield, and the Stars and Stripes.** One particular object of interest is a memorial urn made for George Washington, which marks the first experience of nationwide grief and loss.

A large amount of the folk art on display is by African-American artists. Their work would be an interesting way to view their experiences in early U.S. history as well as the influence of African art and traditions. For any exploration of race relations—past or present—visit this museum. For example, "American Anthem" displays a piece by Mary Smith, "C and W," that portrays two women in exactly the same way except for the colors she used to paint their faces.

Another work by Thornton Dial, Sr., "The Man Rode Past his Barn to Another New Day," depicts a black man on his mule pushing against rope and wire that restrict him to the farm buildings behind him. Dark, grim, and painful, the painting also offers hope and resilience as it explores the experience of African Americans who left behind rural lives for the better opportunity associated with cities. Another amazing painting, also displayed in "American Anthem," is "Hey

Diddle Diddle, Cow Jump Over the Mone" by Nellie Mae Rowe. This shows the artist's face on a cow that's jumping high and freely. An optimist, Rowe experienced the Civil Rights Movement and celebrated its progress.

The exhibit also includes work by such New York City artists as Ralph Fasanella. Fasanella's picture is an interesting homage to his father, an iceman by trade. It shows him crucified on an ice truck in the middle of a New York street. If you'd like to see more of his art, you should visit the 53rd Street subway stop near the museum, where another of his canvases, owned by the city, is on permanent display: a painting of New York City subway riders, appropriately enough.

A book of masterworks from the permanent collection is available to you on each floor of the museum. It's great because it provides an extensive artistic and historic context for each of the works on display in "American Anthem," as well as a few masterworks that did not make it into the exhibit. Take some time to look through this book. The exhibit will make a lot more sense to you, and it is also a great source for taking notes.

Besides checking out the book, the best advice we can give about the museum is TAKE A TOUR. We learned so much! The gallery tour is free to those who have paid the museum's general admission. It not only examines specific pieces of artwork, but also teaches you how to approach folk art—what to look for as you go through the exhibit. Don't be afraid to ask the tour guides questions, especially when you first arrive. They are probably your greatest resource.

Depending on your interests, the museum may offer educational programs that you want to look into. Tours and workshops specifically geared to students are only for large school groups during the school day, and you cannot join a school group that is not your own. But you should look into the many public programs that the museum offers: lectures, films, gallery tours, workshops, artist presentations, and weekend family programs. Many of these are free with admission. You should contact the museum or go online to find current information.

For any questions about using the American Museum of Folk Art as an educational resource, contact Rebecca Hayes at (212) 265-1040 ext. 119.

Notes:

American Museum of the Moving Image

Address:	35th Ave. at 36th St. Astoria, NY 11106
Telephone:	718.784.4520
Directions:	Take the R to Steinway St.
Hours:	Tuesday-Friday 12:00pm-5:00pm
	Saturdays & Sundays 11:00am-6:00pm
	Closed Mondays
Entry Fee:	$4.50 Under 18
Website:	www.ammi.org

No matter what you are writing about, you can probably benefit from a visit to the American Museum of the Moving Image. **Although some topics you may come here to study might be specific to the entertainment industry, you can also gather a lot of information about related issues.** For example, in addition to information on: the oral history of film and the relationships between the major motion picture industries, you can learn about race relations, censorship, licensing, unions, the history of technology, and even patents and antitrust legislation (by studying Edison's contributions to film-making).

The exhibits and archives would both be helpful, but in different ways. The archives will provide you with more detailed information once you have chosen a topic. The majority of the exhibit space that is devoted to the permanent collection focuses more on the process of filmmaking and less on the content of actual films. However, it is worth viewing if you are interested in using movie content in your paper, because it will make you a better film critic. The exhibit traces the development of film from its start in the science of motion study to its current form in both television and movies.

The top floor of the museum concentrates on the technology used to make film and television, while the second floor concentrates on the people involved in that process. You can learn about the different ways sound affects film by voicing over a scene from *Babe, Glory, To Have and Have Not, The Wizard of Oz, or My Fair Lady.* (We were Babe.) Perhaps of greater interest to you, you can choose to play scenes from *Independence Day* and *Romeo and Juliet* with different types of background music to see how different choices of background music affect how you interpret these scenes. Other portions of the exhibit concentrate on light, sound, panning, make-up, costume and too many things to list here.

When we went, the first floor exhibit was "Expanded Entertainment," a large arcade of all sorts of video games (that you can play for free—no additional charge besides the general admission fee) with interesting information about them. (Did you know that Pac-Man was on the cover of *Time* as its 1984 "Man of the Year," or that in 1993 the blood and death in "Mortal Kombat" caused debate in Congress?)

Once you've checked out the lobby exhibit, take a tour of the permanent exhibit "Behind the Screen," especially if you don't know much about film or television or if you're not sure what you're looking for. Though there were some annoying people on my tour, the tour guide was not one of them. He was very knowledgeable and answered questions patiently and thoughtfully. In addition to the exhibits and the archive, the museum offers several programs that might be of interest to you. Though you can't join a school group for activities that occur during the school day, you may join any public programs for adults. These include film screenings and discussions and are worth checking out.

For the most up-to-date information on programs, check the museum's website. It also has online exhibits, including a very interesting one on the history of presidential campaigns on television from 1952 to 1992. You can watch campaign commercials online.

The exhibit also has archives that you might be able to use. Although a large part of the technology that is not on display is stored off-site, the majority of the papers and pictures are at the museum. You may ask the museum about the archives, but keep in mind that they are definitely not where you would start your research. If you do wind up using them, you will most likely be directed to them after completing a significant amount of preliminary research elsewhere.

American Museum of Natural History

Address:	Central Park West & W. 79th St. New York, NY 10024
Telephone:	212.769.5100
Directions:	Take B, C to W. 81st St. Take 1, 9 to Broadway and W. 79th St.
Hours:	Daily 10:00am-5:45pm Fridays Rose Center is open until 8:45pm
Entry Fee:	$9 Students
Website:	www.amnh.org

You may not think the Museum of Natural History will have much to offer for a history paper, but you'll be surprised at what you can find here! **It's great if you have an interest in anthropology, sociology, scientific movements, the history of science** in the United States (which would be a fabulous topic!), **presidents** (mostly Teddy Roosevelt), **explorers** (the library has all of Margaret Mead's books), **space exploration** (at the Rose Center for Earth and Space, a beautiful new facility), **Native American cultures and history, the history of the museum itself, or the role of museums in America or New York.**

Although not all of the exhibits may be relevant to American history, they are fascinating in and of themselves. Whether or not you've already decided on a topic, you may find inspiration in them. They also cover human biology and evolution; geological exhibits; mammals from around the world; plants from around the world; fish from around the world; birds, reptiles, and amphibians (yes, from around the world); and of course the ever-popular dinosaurs. The anthropological exhibits include studies of several Native American groups as well as African, South American, Middle Eastern, and Asian cultures. Perhaps the most impressive of these is the display on the Native American cultures of the Northwest. The masks and totem poles that loom out of the dimly lit hall are worth the trip by themselves.

But wait, there's even more. The museum also puts together special exhibits, to such as one on Albert Einstein and another on the Vietnam War, that could prove useful for research in American history.

To supplement the exhibits, the museum organizes several workshops, lectures, and performances. Many of these programs occur after school and in the evenings and are available to high school students.

Some may require a fee. You should definitely call in advance, since most are on a first-come, first-served basis and have limited space. Recently, a Nobel Prize winner gave an afternoon and an evening lecture. Although you would have been welcome at either one, note that the earlier lectures are typically geared more toward high school students and often include question and answer time. Call or visit the website for a calendar of events.

Once you have been through the exhibits and/or have a focused topic, you should visit the library on the fourth floor. Although it is non-circulating and closed-stack (you cannot take books out!), you can view books from the collection while you are there and make photocopies (for 20 cents a page). You can also photocopy pictures but will have to pay an additional fee and credit the museum when you use them. Some material that is less accessible (because it is fragile or valuable) can only be viewed on slides.

You can call ahead to ask about the library's resources, or look at the catalogue on the Web at www.libcat.amnh.org. Computers are available at the library. Most materials are not related to history, but if your topic concerns natural history or science in any way, it will be a helpful resource.

Check out the Discovery Room on the upper level for hands-on fun. Call to get in, but don't be discouraged by having to make an appointment—it was designed specially for high school students. Here you can do experiments with seismography, use microscopes, and manipulate real data using astrophysics programs on the computers provided. For an additional fee, you can see Imax movies, or if you're really adventurous, you can travel to the ends of the universe and back in the Rose Center's Space Theater. On a side note, **for those of you looking for a job or internship, the museum offers several, both paid and unpaid.**

Never underestimate how much this museum could help your paper. Even information that doesn't at first glance seem to relate directly to your topic could probably be of some use to you. For example, learning about early Native American civilizations and other cultures that helped lay the foundations for modern society is very interesting and will apply to many paper topics.

Stop and look at the commemorative material about Theodore Roosevelt in the Rotunda and the Memorial Hall at the main entrance (the big entry room at the top of the stairs with the really cool dinosaur in the middle of it). Look up at the walls of the Rotunda and read the Roosevelt quotes. The museum put those words up there for a reason. Think about them as you're walking through the exhibits and ask yourself why the institution chose to highlight them as you enter the museum—why, no matter what material you come to study, those words are the first and probably the last thing you see. How do they influence your thoughts as you gather your research? There is an amazing amount of information in the Museum of Natural History; make sure to take advantage of this amazing resource.

Notes:

Notes:

Americas Society

Address:	680 Park Ave. New York, NY 10021
Telephone:	212.628.3200
Directions:	Take the 4, 5, 6 to E. 68th St.
Hours:	See specific events on website
Entry Fee:	See specific events on website
Website:	www.americas-society.org inforequest@as-coa.org

The Americas Society is a fascinating place featuring contemporary art in all media from Central America, South America, and Canada. If you are doing a paper that focuses on the Americas beyond just the United States, the Americas Society will be one of your best resources. If you are tracing any art form (writing, painting, pottery, etc.) or cultural group and want to see both its origin and its development outside the U.S., you cannot find a better place.

The Society features three or four visual arts exhibits a year, covering anything from pre-Colombian to contemporary art, with text panels, reading material at the front desk, and a catalogue. Admission to the gallery is free. Group tours require ten participants, and you must call in advance.

The literature and music departments publish a magazine that includes mostly contemporary writing and artwork from around the Americas, but not the U.S. The music program collaborates with composers and performers from throughout the Western Hemisphere. The visual arts program coordinates events that include concerts, panel discussions, lectures by artists, and readings by authors who also discuss their work with the audience.

Although most of the programs are at the university level, everyone is welcome. Occasionally the Society has talks on public policy, economics, and business, but these may not be relevant to your topic. It also organizes teacher workshops. For a complete listing of programs, visit the website. The Society is willing to work with high school students but doesn't usually do so, so call beforehand to make sure the program(s) you are interested in are appropriate for you.

Notes:

Address:	200 Eastern Parkway Brooklyn, NY 11238
Telephone:	718.638.5000
Directions:	Take 2, 3 to Eastern Parkway/Brooklyn Museum
Hours:	Wednesday-Friday 10:00am-5:00pm
	Saturdays 11:00am-6:00pm
	Closed Mondays & Tuesdays
Entry Fee:	$3 Students
	Free first Saturday of each month
Website:	www.brooklynart.org

You may not be old enough to remember when Brooklyn was its own city, but the Brooklyn Museum of Art remembers. When it first came into being as a small library in 1821, not only had Brooklyn not yet been incorporated into the City of New York, but the Brooklyn Bridge hadn't even been built, and would not be built for another 62 years. **The Brooklyn Museum of Art is unique, because unlike many other world-class institutions** (it is the second biggest museum in the city and holds one of the world's best collections of Egyptian art), **it is very much grounded in its own local history.**

You can come here to study American furniture, architecture, painting, and decorative arts. But you can also come here to study Brooklyn. Indeed, just tracing the history of the museum, which from its start has been an active member of the community, yields an amazing amount of information about the history and development of the borough. **But whether you want to study the history of Brooklyn, the history of New York, or American history in general, the Brooklyn Museum of Art is a great place to visit.**

Don't let the fact that this place is an art museum scare you away. While you will mainly examine different pieces of artwork, there is a great resource center that details all sorts of history behind the exhibits. A few topics you might come to the museum to study include art in or about Brooklyn or New York City, the development of New York City, the museum itself, social activism in the 19th century (building Prospect and Central parks), the role of the museum in American history and society, art from the Atomic Age, early colonial

American artwork (especially the conventions Americans took from the Europeans and the evolution of those conventions into a new American identity), and topics in Native American culture and history.

The majority of the American art on exhibit is part of the museum's permanent collection and grouped together on its own, so it's not hard to find. You should start on the fifth floor at the Luce Center for American Art, where you'll find complimentary audio guides. The current long-term exhibit, "American Identities," mainly includes paintings but also has furniture and sculpture, all relating to the history of the United States. Each room has a designated period, and the rooms are arranged chronologically.

You'll see paintings by Gilbert Stuart, Charles Willson Peale, Samuel F.B. Morse (the telegraph guy was a portrait painter too), and Durand. The East River Park portrait by William Glackens could be used as part of a paper on the importance of parks in an urban environment. In it, you see how life in the park moves at a different pace, as the city's businesses and pollution fade into the background. And be sure to look at "Winter Scene in Brooklyn c. 1819-1820" by Francis Guy. It depicts downtown Brooklyn from a second-story building facing Front Street.

Nearby is an encased antislavery medallion inscribed with the words "Am I not a man and a brother?" which abolitionists put on snuff-boxes and made into jewelry. "Manifest destiny" ring a bell? Well, the progression moves quickly towards works of the Hudson River School and tantalizing depictions of the untamed, seemingly untapped, wilderness that was the West.

An entire room is dedicated to the black image in American art. A video explores works on display as well as other well-known images, such as Aunt Jemima. In the Civil War room, make sure to see "A Ride for Liberty – The Fugitive Slave ca. 1862" by Eastman Johnson. This is a perfect example of how an artwork could be useful in your writing. Johnson traveled during the Civil War, recording his experiences in paintings that he sent to newspapers. This one depicts a black family on horseback pushing to make the Union line in early dawn. Though proud of this painting, Johnson never showed it publicly during his lifetime, because the idea of a black man taking control of his own destiny was too controversial.

Other rooms include works by American artists influenced by Asian art, Native American art, Plain art (folk art), and finally modern art. Probably you will find the last few rooms too abstract and contemporary to be extremely useful, but consider checking them out.

If you want to escape from paintings, visit the fourth floor, where you can find all sorts of American furniture, architecture, and decorative arts. Here entire rooms, in some cases even entire parts of houses, have been reconstructed so that **you can literally walk into the lives of people in different periods and places.** Visit the Hall Jan Martense Schenk house, for example, a two-room house from Flatlands, Brooklyn, ca. 1675. The space you see would have acted as an all-purpose room, including serving as a kitchen. The open hearth, brass, pewter, and earthenware all are typical of the period. Though the room is tidy, so much traffic would have brought in a lot of dirt. If you'd been the person who had to clean the floor, you would have scrubbed the entire thing with sand.

You can also visit the Henry Trippe House from in Secretary, Maryland c. 1730, the Cupola House of Edenton, N.C. (c.1758—the only known example of a Southern house with an overhanging second story), or drop in on John D. Rockefeller in his West 54th Street home.

Disappointed that you're not spending a lot of time in the museum's Egyptian collection? Well, even Egyptian art has influenced American furniture, from pianos, cups, and saucers to lamps. You'll be surprised by what even furniture can tell you. If you are so inspired, you could write an entire paper on the development of styles of American furniture from interpretations of British styles. You could look at pieces of furniture made in the Federal style in 18th-century America and contrast them with their parent style, 18th-century English Chippendale.

If examining the past in houses and paintings isn't enough for you, don't despair. Though it is not currently on display, the museum also has a large collection of Native American artifacts and lots of information on them.

Okay, so now you've got lots of ideas and questions and you're ready to start some hard-core research. Make your way to the learning center, which is free of charge. This place is great, and it was made especially with you in mind. Use it. You need to plan ahead, though, because visiting the center requires an appointment. If you are pretty sure that you'll be doing a large part of your research at the museum, you may want to make an appointment for your first visit rather than having to come back a second time. The number for the learning center is (718) 638-5000 ext. 527. There is also some information about the learning center online at www.bmalearningcenter.org. It is worth your while to click the link to the Brooklyn Expedition, where you'll find a free pass that might prove useful. The learning center is not your best general historical resource, but it's great if you want specific information on objects in the museum's collections.

You can also find information on old and new exhibits. One thing to note is that their inventories also include the text that accompanies each artwork when it is exhibited. So you don't have to spend hours taking notes as you walk through the exhibits - you can just come to the learning center and photocopy the texts. Though there are computers in the learning center for Internet research and CD-ROMs, and photocopying (which is free) is really the best way to take information out of the museum with you, be sure to bring paper and pen - just in case.

In addition to books related to exhibits, **you will find a lot of lesson plans and teacher preparations that will be helpful.** The learning center staff may also direct you to the art reference library or a curatorial department, but you should not try to contact them on your own. If you are directed to them, you will have to make a request in writing and wait for staff to contact you before you can visit.

The museum runs many programs that you should consider taking advantage of: art classes for students in which you explore the museum's holdings and learn how to view and create art; several teen programs; a student critics institute, where you discuss contemporary artwork in the museum; and a summer apprentice program where you learn about art by preparing to lead younger students through the museum. For information and fees, check the museum's website.

Perhaps more helpful for doing research and more convenient for your schedule are "first Saturday" programs. Although the museum lets you pay what you wish, on the first Saturday of every month it doesn't ask for any admission fee and offers **several special programs, including concerts, performances, artist talks, curator-led tours of exhibits, films, and even parties—all free**. If you can't make a first Saturday, don't worry. Tours of the different galleries are given throughout the week and are free with admission. Special programs also occur on other weekend days other than the first Saturday.

The changing exhibits may or may not be relevant to your research topic. To find out about them, you should check out the museum's website.

Cooper-Hewitt, National Design Museum

Address:	2 E. 91st St. New York, NY
Telephone:	212.849.8400
Directions:	Take the 4,5,6 to E. 86th or E. 96th St. stations
Hours:	Tuesdays 10:00am-9:00pm
	Wednesday-Friday 10:00am-5:00pm
	Saturdays 10:00am-6:00pm
	Sundays 12:00am-6:00pm
	Closed Mondays and federal holidays
Entry Fee:	$5 Students Free Tuesdays 5:00pm-9:00pm
Website:	www.ndm.si.edu

The Cooper-Hewitt National Design Museum is not a research source for everyone. It is fun to visit, though, and it offers several design programs that you might be interested in, even if you're not thinking of writing a paper on design. Does helping to create shoes for Nike or rides for Disney theme parks sound exciting? Read on. To come here specifically for research, you really need a topic that has to do with art, design, or architecture... or Andrew Carnegie. (His former mansion is now the museum building.)

If your paper is in fact about art, design, architecture, or Andrew Carnegie, then this is the place to be. **The museum is especially strong in anything relating to the history of design, decorative arts, and the role of design in everyday life.** To get you started, you should consider taking a tour of the building or of the exhibits, but be warned: you need to call at least two weeks in advance. Also, you'll need at least eight people.

We'd recommend walking into the first floor of the museum and sitting at the large table under the staircase that leads up to the second floor. On the table are several copies of a book about the exhibits on display. This book is comprehensive and gives background information that the text panels do not provide. After you've taken notes, walk through the exhibits and spend time on the items in the book that seemed particularly interesting to you. The museum only has two small floors, and while these exhibits are fascinating, they will be valuable to you only after you've read up about them.

Since Cooper-Hewitt is by no means a history museum, in order to make use of it, you must approach the information creatively. While nothing on display in the museum will necessarily provide a topic for your research paper, everything can be used in some way. This is to say, you may not be doing a paper on the history of American kitchenware, but knowing some facts about it could be helpful in studying a topic like the American home front during World War II.

Creativity lends itself to papers that are fun and interesting both to read and to write. So go crazy here—have some fun with the exhibits and look to the research opportunities (see next paragraph) to help you incorporate the exhibits into your paper. Cooper-Hewitt is a unique museum whose exhibits may be sparse in terms of context, but it has great research resources.

What you should pay attention to at Cooper-Hewitt are the research opportunities and the school programs. You can research stuff in the museum's collection that is not on display in addition to researching what is on display. To start, call the Study Center at (212) 849-8385. Although you'll need an appointment, the Study Center is free and it's open to everyone. You should have an idea of what you want to look at when you call so that the educators can have material ready for you.

The depth of the collection to which you have access is really astounding. Pieces date from the time of ancient Greece to the present day. To give you an idea of the enormity and the greatness of the museum's collections, you can look at its four curatorial departments: Applied Arts and Industrial Design, Drawings and Prints, Textiles, and Wall Coverings. The Applied Arts and Industrial Design division consists of over 40,000 three-dimensional objects. These objects include chairs, lighting fixtures, tablewares, gates, match safes, buttons, and birdcages.

The museum holds more than 160,000 works of art in its Drawings and Print Division, dating from the Renaissance to the present day. These designs are for the decorative arts, ornaments, gardens, jewelry, theater, interiors, graphic and industrial design, and even the fine arts. A 30,000-piece textile division includes embroidery, knitting, braiding, quilting, knotting, crochet, needlework, bobbin lace, dyed fabrics, and woven fabrics. A 10,000-piece wall covering division is the best collection of its kind in the country. It contains wall coverings from the wealthiest homes to the simplest. Be it gilded leather, block print, patterned, or scenic print, there are examples of it.

This collection may be daunting due to its size, but it offers a wealth of information. One thing you should note is that many objects come from foreign countries, and date back to the time before the U.S. existed. If you are tracing the emergence of an American tradition and need to look beyond American design to see its origins and its influences, the non-U.S. part of the collection could be really useful to you.

A word of advice: though each curatorial division has its own phone number for appointments, which you can get online, don't call them first. Start at the Study Center and let them direct you to the curatorial divisions. You will get a much better reception from the curators this way.

We mentioned educational programs. **Of all the programs at the museums that we have visited, the Cooper-Hewitt's are among the best.** For example, Design Directions, aimed at high school kids interested in design, was based on the idea that students should be able to come in on their own. So programs are scheduled around the school day, and you can participate for free (if you are a New York City public school student). Design Directions offers Design Days, one-day hands-on workshops with professional designers; Design Studios, multi-session after-school workshops with professional designers; Portfolio Workshops, where a panel of college professors and admissions officers discusses how to create design portfolios for college and your later career; college and university visits and application workshops, which are one-day sessions that explore opportunities for studying design at the college level; studio visits—you go visit actual designers' workplaces—and internships, which are 10-week work opportunities in different design studios.

In the past, **Design Direction workshops have paired students with designers to create a clothing line for the Gap, rides for Disney theme parks, on-air promos for MTV, websites about contemporary global issues for the Internet company Concrete Media, shoes for Nike, and plans for the future of the Washington Heights neighborhood.** In 2003, students in Design Directions will help plan the rebuilding of downtown New York.

All of these programs are first-come, first-served, so call to reserve yourself a place in the ones that interest you as soon as you can. We would definitely recommend taking advantage of these programs, especially those relevant to your research topic. To find out about the newest Design Direction programs or to register, call (212) 849-8390.

The museum also offers a weeklong design institute in July that you might consider incorporating into your summer plans. In addition, there are also adult programs. Those, however, are not free and can be rather expensive. If there is an adult program that is of particular interest to you, ask if the museum will cover the cost for you. There is no guarantee that they will be able to do this, but if they can, they will.

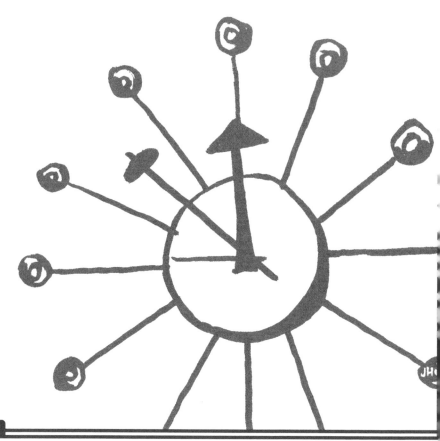

Address:	1 E. 70th St. New York, NY 10021
Telephone:	212.288.0700
Directions:	Take the 6 to E. 68th St.
Hours:	Tuesday-Thursday & Saturdays 10:00am-6:00pm
	Fridays 10:00am-9:00pm
	Closed Mondays
Entry Fee:	$5 Students
Website:	www.frick.org

The Frick Collection is a major museum of European paintings from the 14th to 19th centuries. It includes such masters as Rembrandt, Vermeer, Van Dyck, El Greco, Renoir, and Gainsborough. Only two American painters are represented in the collection: Gilbert Stuart and James McNeil Whistler. The museum also includes furniture and sculpture.

It is true that such an art collection by itself would not be very helpful in researching topics from American history. **However, the house and the collection offer a unique perspective into the life and times of Henry Clay Frick, a man who made his money in Pittsburgh coke and steel, and who chose to spend the end of his life in Gilded Age New York City.**

Frick was born in 1849 on a Pennsylvania farm, far from the life of the big city. Denied a substantial inheritance, he set out to build his future in the coal industry. He supplied coke (compressed coal) to Pittsburgh's burgeoning steel industry and became a millionaire by age thirty. At this point, Frick had both the interest and the funds to begin collecting art. He traveled to Europe with his close friend Andrew Mellon and purchased a great deal of art. Not a typical collector of his time, he bought what he liked, regardless of current fashion. **Almost exclusively portraiture and landscapes, the paintings in his collection and how they are displayed reflect his life and the time in which he lived.**

When you come to the Frick, be sure to look not only at the paintings but also at the entire house. Thomas Hastings, who also designed the New York Public Library, built it. The interior was constructed specifically to accommodate the collection. Each room is arranged to allow for the best viewing of the paintings and sculpture. Unlike a typical museum, the rooms here have been left more or less in their original arrangements; this affords you the privilege of moving around the rooms essentially unrestricted. The house has been expanded since its construction, and some paintings have been added since Frick's death, but all has been done in keeping with the tenor of the residence.

When you visit the Frick, you should definitely pick up an "acoustiguide" recording, which is free with admission. And be sure to check out the Frick Library. Built by his daughter after his death, this nearby thirteen story structure houses one of the best art research libraries in the world. Although it concentrates primarily on European art, you should be aware of this valuable resource. While you do not need an official appointment, you should still call to make sure that the library is able to accommodate you. If you have any questions about the collection, contact Amy Herman, Director of Education, at (212) 547-6856, or go online and e-mail the collection.

Notes:

Address:	287 Convent Ave. New York, NY 10005
Telephone:	212.283.5154
Directions:	Take the C to 145th St. or 1, 9 to 137th St.
Hours:	Friday-Sunday 9:00am-5:00pm Closed Monday-Thursday
Entry Fee:	Free admission
Website:	www.nps.gov/hagr
Education Contact:	212.666.1640

Alexander Hamilton? If you're thinking, "Oh, no, not another founding father! Like we haven't already studied enough about these guys"– think again. This one is really interesting, and visiting **Hamilton Grange, his house, is a great way to learn about Hamilton, pre-Revolutionary America, America during the Revolution, the nation's first years as a republic, early New York City history, and even colonial period furniture and architecture. But what should really fascinate you is Hamilton himself.** If you want to write about someone who will baffle and amaze you, visit Hamilton Grange and find new appreciation for the house's original owner.

So why is Alexander Hamilton so interesting? Here is some background to get you started. Talk about the self-made man. His father was James Hamilton, a nobleman with the title of Scottish Lord of the Grange. But Alexander Hamilton's young life wasn't a picnic. He was born out of wedlock in the West Indies, and his father abandoned him, his brother, and his mother when Alexander was only ten.

By the time Hamilton was twelve, his mom had died, and he'd begun supporting himself by clerking in a commercial firm in St. Croix. After putting himself through school and running the shop while its owner was away for months at a time, Hamilton earned a reputation as a standout. He was so good that his boss didn't give him any flak for firing the firm's lawyer during one of the boss's long absences.

When Hamilton published an article about a 1772 hurricane, so many citizens were impressed by his talents that they funded a trip to New York to continue his education. By the age of nineteen, he had graduated from King's College (now Columbia University) and was poised to study law. In college Hamilton had taken a great interest in politics and spoke publicly for the first time in defense of the Boston Tea Party in 1773—when he was only 18! During the Revolutionary War, George Washington was impressed by Hamilton's military and intellectual abilities and soon made him a close advisor.

Did you know that he pushed to give blacks the right to fight in the Revolution, or that after the war he founded the New York Manumission Society to encourage slaveholders to free their slaves? He himself never owned slaves; rather, he paid the few servants who worked for him. Attributing his hatred of slavery to encounters with it in his childhood, Hamilton never forgot the region where he was born. While engaged in U.S. politics, he found time to produce a practical plan for Toussaint L'Ouverture's government in Haiti and encouraged Haiti's successful slave revolt against the French.

Hamilton was the only New Yorker to sign the Constitution. He was also the main contributor to the Federalist Papers, which explained and championed the Constitution. As the first Secretary of the U. S. Treasury, Hamilton dealt with the national debt by insisting that government war bonds be repaid at full price. This established the government's credibility and encouraged more citizens to buy bonds, since they were paid back with interest. The government used the money to pay back loans and invest in industries that would generate long-term wealth. Hamilton also established the Federal Bank of the United States and used his authority to encourage business and better diplomatic relations with England.

Hamilton also started the *New York Post* and ran a lucrative law practice. When he died from a gunshot incurred in a duel, he was only 49. He was a complex character study until his death: even though Hamilton helped outlaw dueling in New York, he couldn't refuse Burr's challenge, so he and Burr went to New Jersey to duel. (Such a law-abiding citizen.) Imagine what more he might have done had he only lived, say, ten more years!

All right. So what about the house that Hamilton lived in? Well, first, he didn't really live there. He didn't commission the house until he had finished his political career, and it wasn't completed until 1802. The family primarily rented apartments in downtown Manhattan so that Hamilton could be near the capitol building (Federal Hall—another National Park Service site you might want to visit) and his law practice. Once the house was built and his family moved, Hamilton was still practicing law and spent most of his time downtown.

But he did occasionally do business in the house, and the first floor is restored to show how he and his family would have used the space, including accurate reproductions of furniture. When you walk up to the first floor, you should notice the unique symmetry of the house, including the two large octangular rooms whose walls are not all equal in size, an unusual way to proportion a room in that period.

Aside from Hamilton, you could learn a lot here about period architecture. Unfortunately, only the first floor of the house is both restored and open to the public. However, you can see everything: grand entryway, office, dining room, sitting room, and two guest bedrooms, which hosted such visitors as Abigail Adams, Napoleon's brother, Gouveneur Morris, and Chancellor Kent. The basement floor is also open, but not restored. Instead, it holds several text panels about the house and about Hamilton. A plus: it's air conditioned, so if you visit the first floor in the heat you can always retreat downstairs to cool off.

After the Hamiltons left the house, it changed owners several times before being donated to St. Luke's Episcopal Church in 1889 and being moved a few blocks to its current location. Parts of the house were rearranged; thus, seeing its "unique symmetry" takes a little imagination. The Park Service hopes to restore all of the house and move it again to nearby St. Nicholas Park, a more rural environment like that of its earlier days.

Although it may not seem so when you first walk into Hamilton Grange, there is a lot of useful information here for you. Start in the basement with the exhibits on the house and on Hamilton. Ask the ranger about the tours and the slide shows, which will supply you with a great deal of information you'd miss on your own. This is not a great place to try a self-guided tour, since there are no text panels at all on the first floor. Usually the tours run every hour on the hour, and the slide shows run in the middle of the day on the half hour. Just make sure that the park site is open when you decide to visit. Currently, Hamilton Grange is only open on Fridays, Saturdays, and Sundays.

A small reference library includes a book of sketches of how all the rooms would have looked when the Hamiltons lived in them, including the second-floor rooms, which you can't go up and see. You should call ahead to see if any library material would be useful for what you are studying. Your best resources are the rangers. Pick their brains. They know a lot about the house and about Alexander Hamilton and are more than happy to help you.

An additional note: the ranger we spoke with mentioned that **the National Park Service has sites in New York City, particularly related to naval defense of the New York City area, that represent every major period from the colonial era through the 20th century. New York City's involvement in war and its naval defense might be an interesting topic. Also, you can usually find out a lot about the neighborhoods surrounding the different National Park Service sites,** how communities have changed over time. Such a topic, or the similar one of urban renewal, might be of interest to you. For questions about different National Park Service sites in and around New York City, call the Gateway National Recreation Area at Fort Wadsworth, which is the location of the Education Center for the National Park Service in the New York City area, at (718) 354-4500.

Address:	441 Clarke Ave. Staten Island, NY 10306
Telephone:	718.351.1611
Directions:	Take the Staten Island Ferry then the S74 to Richmond Rd. and St. Patrick's Place
Hours:	September-June: Wednesday-Sunday 1:00pm-5:00pm
	June-August: Mondays & Wednesday-Saturday 10:00am-5:00pm Sundays 1:00pm-5:00pm
Entry Fee:	$3.50 Under 17 $5.00 Over 17
Website:	www.historicrichmondtown.org

Okay, so it's a trek. But it's worth it. Unlike any of the other museums in this guide, **Historic Richmond Town is a living museum. When you visit, you find out what life was like in the late 17th, 18th, and early 19th centuries because you don't examine the houses and artifacts, you meet individuals.** These are people who, dressed in period costume, show you how they would have made a living in the houses over a century ago.

The museum's earliest building dates back to 1695, when it was inhabited by Hendrick Kroesen and his young family. Historic Richmond Town was one of the earliest Dutch settlements on the island, and because of its central location it became the center for the Dutch Reformed Church on Staten Island.

The church couldn't afford a minister until 1701, so Hendrick Kroesen served as the community's *voorlezer* (lay minister) and schoolteacher from 1696 to 1701. Walk into his house and visit the schoolroom where he would have taught his pupils, as well as the small room in the back where he and his young family would have slept, eaten, and done most of their housework, since it was easier to heat just one room.

Visit the Boehm House and hear about its construction and the tools used to build it. Learn how to date a building by looking at such minute details as the shape of the nails holding the house together and the type of molding and paneling used to decorate it. Visit the Bennett House to see an exhibit on "Home-Life in the 1880s." Visit the Guyon Tavern, the Carpenter Shop, the Print Shop, and the Tinsmith Shop to see people demonstrate their trades. Learn how cooking would have been done in the Guyon-Lake-Tysen House. Also, check out the houses of both tradesmen and farmers and notice the differences between them.

As you walk through the different buildings, ask questions about the houses, the people who would have lived in them, their clothing, and their furniture, and **think about how they would have had to perform their daily tasks without the modern conveniences that today we take for granted. Think about social class, trade, and gender roles. Think about which house and which lifestyles seem most and least attractive to you and why.** This is a great place to get ideas and to home in on them.

Also, be sure to look at houses that are not currently open to the public. Information on all the buildings, regardless of whether they are open to the public, is available to you in the museum's library, probably your best resource at Richmond Town. Though small and focused on Staten Island history, it holds a rich assortment of local historical information. **If you are doing a paper on anything from colonial days through the Civil War and the Victorian era, come here and see how people experienced those periods on a local level, in areas such as architecture, building construction, businesses, clothing, decorative arts, letters, trades, the military, and daily life.** Some of the library's documents include papers freeing local slaves in 1827, when New York State officially abolished all slavery.

The library contains three sets of diaries: one from 1850, written by the Merrell sisters; one from the late 1800's that spans about ten years, written by Ida Dudley Dale, a child from a middle-class family; and the Cutting Diaries, which date from the 1880s. These can teach you a lot. Learn what life was like for Ida as she came of age, and notice that as late as the 1880s, the farmer who writes about his daily routine does not even mention Christmas.

The library has a fascinating collection of photographs, many of which were taken by Alice Austen, an upper-middle-class woman who did not have to work until the stock market crashed in 1929. Her pictures include several of parlors, girls' bedrooms, friends, Staten Island, Manhattan, and people such as the policemen and street cleaners she encountered as she walked around the greater New York area. Her photographs even include shots of the Columbian Exposition, Vermont, Maryland, and Chicago.

Other holdings include the Santoro Collection of Italian American artifacts, two World War I collections and one World War II collection, and material from the Civil War and the Revolutionary War. In addition, the library has a lot of information on linoleum. Bet you didn't know that the first linoleum factory in the United States was on Staten Island. Now named Travis, the town where the factory was built was first named Linoleumville. You will also find information on Prohibition Park, now Westerleigh, which was originally a community put together by temperance families.

You'll need an appointment to use this library, but the librarian, Carlotta Defillo, is very eager to work with fine high school students like you, so give her a call at (718) 351-1611 ext. 299. Let her know ahead of time what you are interested in looking at. Leave her a message with your name, number, and your topic(s) of interest, and she will be happy to return your call. Using the library is free, but you might have to spend some money on photocopying.

There are several educational programs that you might be able to take advantage of, depending on how much time you have. **During the summer, apprenticeships and internships are offered.** As an apprentice you will work in costume with a master and learn a skill such as cooking, tin-smithing, coopering and turning, dressmaking, millinery, needlecrafts, or basket making. You will also learn the historical background of the skill and the building you are assigned to. The shortest apprenticeship lasts three weeks, by which time you are expected to show basic proficiency in your skill. You can stay longer and hone your skills even more. As an intern you will also be in costume, but you'll be discussing the different buildings with visitors as you learn how to interpret them rather than displaying a trade. The Education Department is also willing to offer a research-based internship, which would mainly involve working with the archives in the library, although such an internship does not yet exist.

The Education Department is revamping its activities for school-aged visitors. It now works mainly with lower and middle schools but can adapt projects to fit a high school audience. Four projects in particular that would fit a high school audience are "Acting as Citizens," where visitors explore the role of individual citizens within the Richmond Town community; "You Be the Judge," in which students reenact county court scenarios from the 19th century in the 1837 courthouse; "Fiber to Thread," where visitors learn about how fibers were made into threads, dyed, made into cloth, and then laundered, back before industrialization; and "Trash or Treasure?" where visitors explore what artifacts can tell them about a building's history.

Unfortunately, many of the programs are meant for groups. However, if you can't get a group together, the Education Department can still send you information. Dial the main number, (718) 351-1611, and ask for the Education Department.

In addition to programs aimed specifically at students, Historic Richmond Town also has several activities that may be interesting alternatives to traditional research. Past events include a Civil War Weekend; a Bluegrass Festival; Old Home Day, when several traditional crafts and skills were demonstrated; and a lecture by Laurel Thatcher Ulrich, a Harvard professor and noted author of *The Age of Homespun,* who discussed how objects can tell stories about American history. Historic Richmond Town also holds traditional dinners in December and candle-lit tours that focus on the history of Christmas. Also, in addition to the general tours currently available, by the spring Historic Richmond Town hopes to give themed tours of the community.

Another resource is the Staten Island Historical Society. While there are no research opportunities for high school students, it does have several exhibits that may be of interest to you, as well as a small video about Historic Richmond Town that is a good introduction to the community.

Most of the introduction to Historic Richmond Town found in the video can also be found on the website. We would recommend you check it out to see if the town will be useful to you before devoting the time it takes to get there.

Intrepid Sea-Air-Space Museum

Address:	Pier 86, 12th Ave. & 46th St. New York, NY 10036
Telephone:	212.245.0072
Directions:	Take any train to 42nd St., then the M42(bus) to the Hudson River
Hours:	Spring/Summer: Monday–Friday 10:00am-5:00pm Saturdays, Sundays & Holidays 10:00am-7:00pm Fall/Winter: Tuesday–Sunday 10:00am-5:00pm Closed Mondays Holidays 10:00am-5:00pm
Entry Fee:	$10 Students
Website:	www.intrepidmuseum.org

Please note: The museum is handicap-accessible, but the U.S.S. *Growler* and *Edson* are not.

The Intrepid Museum can be an excellent resource for your paper, but a simple description of the museum fails to convey the thrill of stepping onto the decks of a ship that's as long as three football fields and covered with some of the most impressive aircraft ever built. You'll feel exhilarated and maybe intimidated. The scale of the scene seems too impressive to be the construct of human hands. Equally impressive is the fact that the men who operated the ship were able to accelerate an airplane (a multi-ton chunk of metal) from zero to 100 in less than two seconds.

The simple fact that the *Intrepid* is still afloat is a testament to the ingenuity and resilience of the American navy. The ship has withstood several attacks, including hours on fire following the second of two kamikaze assaults. She has also survived several bombings and a torpedo strike. In short, even if you are scared of the water, or for that matter, of bombs, fire, and kamikazes, you'll still feel safe on board the *Intrepid.*

The *Intrepid* was a working aircraft carrier in both World War II and the Vietnam War. It was decommissioned in 1974 and became a museum in 1982. The primary exhibit is, of course, the ship itself. On the top level are many of the aircraft from its days of service. **Inside the ship, displays range from early flight to early submarines to the development of the space program.**

Also docked at Pier 86 are the U.S.S. *Growler* SSG-577 and *Edson* DD-946. The *Growler* is the only guided missile submarine in the world open to the public. The *Edson* is a destroyer from the same era as the *Intrepid*. There are tours available of both these vessels, and free audio guides available at the ticket office. Be sure to get one! Where the exhibits are lacking in background information, these guides prove very helpful. There are also tours at regular intervals that go through the exhibits. The tour guides are extremely knowledgeable and friendly and will be good resources for you. There is a film meant to introduce the museum, but it is hardly worth the eight minutes unless you've missed all the U.S. military ads on T.V.

There are several "hidden" resources that the museum offers but does not advertise. Among these are a library, classroom space, workshops, and computers with Internet access and word processing—all open for you to use. The staff is more than happy to work with you and is glad to have you join any of their school programs. While most of these are geared to students younger than you, there are also teacher workshops designed for adults, which might prove useful. They cover a range of topics in 20th-century American history, with a focus on military history. To find out about these programs or to set up an appointment to speak with a staff member, call Allison Laufer, Associate Director of Education, at (212) 245-0072 ext. 8052. She has offered to try to arrange interviews for you with veterans, some of whom served on the *Intrepid* when it was in service.

Address:	1109 Fifth Ave. at 92nd St. New York, NY 10128
Telephone:	212.423.3200
Directions:	Take the 4,5,6 to E. 86th St.
Hours:	Sundays 10:00am-5:45pm
	Monday-Wednesday 11:00am-5:45pm
	Thursdays 11:00am-8:00pm
	Fridays 11:00am-3:00pm
	Closed Saturdays
Entry Fee:	$5.50 Students
	Thursdays 5-8 Pay what you wish
Website:	www.jewishmuseum.org

The Jewish Museum focuses on the American Jewish experience, especially in New York. In the process, it covers a lot of the history of New York and the United States.

While two of its four floors are dedicated to the permanent collection, a comprehensive history of Judaism that includes artifacts from all over the world, the remaining two floors host exhibits that may or may not have to do with Judaism. For example, we saw an exhibit entitled "New York: Capital of Photography" that consisted of pictures of New York from the advent of photography to the present day.

The museum does offer a lot of educational classes, but they're for groups of up to 30 students, they're run during the school day, and they cost $55.00. If you're on your own, the education department suggests that you call them with any questions after you have looked through the museum and the website. They cannot meet with you one-on-one, but, realizing that you can't come to a class unless you somehow convince your teacher to take your entire class on a field trip (worth a try if you're up to it), the museum educators have agreed to meet with groups of at least five students. If you call ahead to discuss a specific topic, be prepared to tell them what kind of information you're looking for so they can look through their stuff and prepare to answer questions during your appointment.

You can ask about anything that is or has been on display, or an issue that the museum has dealt with in its exhibits. Before you go, it would be a good idea to check out past exhibits and other general information on the website. To give you an idea of just a few of the things you can ask about, the following are some topics on which museum educators have already taught and compiled a great amount of material: "Examining Identity through TV and Popular Culture" using television clips to discuss how TV shapes our ideas of culture. "Understanding the Holocaust through Art and Artifacts" with a significant amount of U.S. history, including the United States' involvement in World War II and the formation of Israel; and "Paintings Tell Stories," using paintings in the museum's collection to teach about the American Jewish experience.

Other programs include "Immigration to America" and "Bridges and Boundaries," which compares the Jewish-American and African-American experiences. No matter what you are studying, don't count out the Jewish Museum. They just might have information on it. It's worth it to call and find out if they can help you with your research.

The Education Department said that the best way to use the museum is really just to come in on your own and view the exhibits. Whether or not you have a topic in mind, that's a great way to get information. And while the museum focuses on art and not history, the text panels in the exhibits tend to give a great deal of historical information about the different artifacts.

The permanent exhibit on Judaism contains a great deal of U.S. history. While the majority of artifacts that relate to American history are from the last 100 years, several date back as far as the founding of our country. One object of note is an 1808 portrait of Sally Etting, a young girl from a wealthy Jewish family that immigrated to Baltimore at the turn of the 19th century. Another section of the exhibit presents the views of different Jewish leaders on slavery. You can find out which groups opposed it, which defended the status quo, and why.

To help you navigate your way through the exhibits, you might consider taking a tour. They're free with admission and always add interesting detail and perspective. We would especially recommend tours if you are walking through an exhibit you know very little about. The guides are great—they add information to the text panels and highlight different parts of the exhibit. Also available for many of the exhibits are audio guides. They are free with admission and are available on the floor of each exhibit.

We would recommend reading the website's information about exhibits before you go to the museum. As further impetus to check out the website, you should know that the museum occasionally puts discount admission ticket offers there. All you have to do is print out the page with the offer and give it to the cashier when you buy your ticket.

When you enter the museum, be sure to look for brochures about current public programs and an updated museum calendar. Although there may be a fee for public programs, they tend to be related to the special exhibits, so if you enjoy an exhibit you may consider trying the program.

If you are still looking for additional research information, consider teacher workshops. Call and find out whether you can attend and whether the content is relevant to your topic. Also, check out the gift shop for titles of books that might be helpful to you. You can probably find any of the gift shop's books at the library.

The museum also has a resource center, which includes a broadcast archive. Ideally, this would be the place to do research. Unfortunately, the museum is undergoing renovations at the moment, and that includes the resource center. Renovations should be completed by the end of the 2002-2003 school year.

The research center was designed with kids like you in mind. The broadcast archive might be of particular interest to you, no matter what you're studying. It reflects the huge involvement of Jews in the entertainment industry and includes all types of shows. Although the shows deal heavily with Jewish American culture, they also cover many other aspects of American culture that may be relevant to your topic.

For any questions about how to research at the museum, call Michelle Asch, the Manager for Schools and Outreach, at (212) 423-3231.

Notes:

Lower East Side Tenement Museum

Address:	90 Orchard St. New York, NY 10002
Telephone:	212.431.0233
Directions:	Take the F to Delancey St. or the J, M, Z to Essex
Hours:	Monday-Sunday 11:00am-5:30pm
	Tours: See website
Entry Fee:	$7 Students
Website:	www.tenement.org

When you walk into the Lower East Side Tenement Museum, you walk into the lives of immigrants who lived more than 100 years ago. The tour of 97 Orchard Street (one of the first tenements built on the Lower East Side, dating from 1864) leads you through the reconstructed apartments of some of its inhabitants. The building was constructed by Lukas Glockner and served as a home to 7,000 immigrants from 20 different countries during the 71 years the building was maintained. It fell into disrepair after stricter building codes forced its closing in 1935, but the museum has since renovated it.

The renovation included restoring four apartments to the way they appeared when families lived there from the 1860s through the 1930s. The tour first brings you to an apartment that's in the same condition as it was when the renovations began. Then you go across the hall into the home of the Gumpertz family, where Julia Gumpertz raised her two daughters by taking up sewing after her husband disappeared. The tour then goes upstairs to the home of the Rogarshevskys, a Lithuanian Orthodox Jewish family. The apartment resembles the way it looked when the family sat shiva (mourned) for their father and husband.

Another large family lived across the hall: the Confinos, a middle-class couple who fled Greece in 1913. Keep in mind that these people hoped to find a better life in America but ended up in a tiny, rat-infested apartment that they shared with their six children. The Baldizzis, who lived upstairs, arrived in 1928 but were forced to move out when the building closed in 1935. Their apartment was reconstructed largely according to the memories shared by a woman who grew up there. The family moved to America in hopes of finding wealth, only to be confronted by the Great Depression. Nevertheless, the memories of Josephine Baldizzi, which you can hear via tape recorder, are happy ones.

This is an excellent place to visit if you are studying a wide range of topics related to the period when this building was occupied. **Make sure to come here if you are researching immigration, housing or safety laws, New York City history, and/or the Great Depression.** A number of artifacts may be of interest. For example, in the Rogarshevsky apartment there are several old medicinal tools and substances used to treat Mr. Rogarshevsky, who died of turberculosis.

Although the museum is rather small and does not offer many programs, it does sponsor special programs on occasion. For example, some days there are people dressed up as the individuals who lived in the apartments. These actors are trained to answer questions from the point of view of immigrants and could be a valuable research tool. You can also take a walking tour of the neighborhood, led by a museum tour guide.

You should definitely visit the website if you are unable to visit the museum in person. The site contains almost the entire tour, with several pictures and videos of the apartments and helpful background information about them.

Notes:

Metropolitan Museum of Art

Address:	1000 Fifth Ave. at 82nd St. New York, NY 10028
Telephone:	212.535.7710
Directions:	Take the 4,5, or 6 to 86th St.
Hours:	Sundays & Tuesday-Thursday 9:30am-5:30pm Fridays & Saturdays 9:30am-9:00pm Closed Mondays
Entry Fee:	$7 Students
Website:	www.metmuseum.org

The Met is a great place to begin research and one of the best places to come up with an idea for a project if you don't have one yet. Not only does it house a huge collection of American art and artifacts from the mid-17th century to the turn of the 20th, but it also has a lot of historical resources about these pieces in its libraries.

The museum's collection includes everything from the exterior of an early 19th-century Wall Street bank to rooms furnished in the styles of cities along the Eastern seaboard in different periods; from individual pieces of pewter, silver, and glass to clothes, musical instruments, and an astounding collection of American paintings, sculpture, drawings, prints, decorative arts, furniture, and photographs. Since the opening of the Henry R. Luce Center for the Study of American Art, the American art displayed in the American Wing has become accessible to the public year-round.

The American Collection is one of the few in the museum that you can see in their entirety at any given time. The only pieces not present are on loan or undergoing restoration. Items on display are grouped by theme or period and arranged to provide interesting and thought-provoking comparisons in style, in period, or between artists. Works by American artists born after 1875 are housed in the Modern Art galleries. There are also American pieces in several galleries around the museum, such as Musical Instruments, Arms and Armor, and Costumes.

Besides the galleries, the Met also has several libraries. The best one for high school students is the Library and Teacher Resource Center in the Uris Center for Education. It contains a listing of all of the objects the Met owns, as well as additional material that helps put the object you are looking at into its proper historical context. Nearly all of the museum's American art is described in volumes written by the curators. You can also look at teaching materials. But don't leave yet; there are also several videos and short films you can watch at the library. While you can't take any materials home with you, you can photocopy them for a minimal fee. Also in the library are bulletins that the museum puts out five times a year, highlighting its acquisitions and related news. This library is open to you. In fact, it even caters to students, especially those in junior high and high school. Best of all, the library is free.

You should also look into the museum's classes. They run on a trimester schedule in the fall, summer, and spring. They're free but do require pre-registration. Ranging from beginner to advanced levels, they cover everything from conversation about art and art history to drawing and painting. Also, you are welcome to attend any of the concerts, workshops, or lectures that are advertised to adults. You may need to pre-register. Like the classes, these are free. Both the classes and workshops are excellent ways to narrow down general interests to a more specific focus suitable for a paper. Once you begin to look at individual pieces in the collection, be sure to note their accession numbers and look them up in the Luce Center computers, for information on the objects and the artists who created them.

Of particular note is the Met's collection of paintings by Thomas Eakins, Winslow Homer, and several Hudson River School painters. It includes several paintings by Thomas Cole, as well as *The Heart of the Andes* by Frederic Edwin Church and *The Rocky Mountains, Lander's Peak* by Albert Bierstadt. Also in the collection are Thomas Hovenden's *The Last Moments of John Brown,* Gilbert Stuart's portrait of Washington (the image of him that has since been used on the one-dollar bill), and *Washington Crossing the Delaware* by Emanuel Gottlieb Leutze—all on view in the American Wing.

A simple list of names cannot convey the emotional impact of these works. *Washington Crossing the Delaware* is especially evocative. Housed in a room with many other seminal works by other painters, Leutze's masterpiece overshadows them all due to its sheer size and its stirring portrayal. The nearly life-sized Washington stands in the prow of his boat, a veritable pillar of fortitude. The icebergs, rendered in exquisite detail, seem as sharp and menacing today as they must have appeared to the soldiers in that boat so long ago. Sitting before this painting, one cannot help but feel the pride and patriotism of those men on that day.

Other permanent American holdings of the museum include architectural works by Louis Comfort Tiffany and Frank Lloyd Wright. A clear contrast can be seen between Wright's 1914 designs and the furniture of a colonial Massachusetts room from 1650, and you'd be amazed how interesting it might be to write a paper that contrasts the two. In 2003 a new exhibit opens: "African-American Artists, 1929-1945: Prints, Drawings, and Paintings from the Metropolitan Museum of Art." It joins a rotating exhibit of American drawings and watercolors. Remember that the museum, while displaying art from cultures all around the world, was founded by American artists and maintains a sizable, multi-faceted American collection.

For more information about the museum, you can contact anyone in the education department at (212) 570-3961. Alice Schwarz has volunteered her name as someone who would be more than willing to help you navigate your way through the museum. Also, the website is very helpful.

Notes:

Address:	Roger Morris Park, 65 Jumel Terrace (at W. 160th St.) New York, NY 10032
Telephone:	212.923.8008
Directions:	Take the C to W. 163rd St. & Amsterdam Ave.
Hours:	Wednesday-Sunday 10:00am-4:00pm Mondays & Tuesdays to groups only
Entry Fee:	$2 Students
Website:	www.preserve.org/hht/morris/jumel.htm

Imagine an elegant summerhouse built just 11 miles from the city, on a hill from which New Jersey, Connecticut, and all of the New York harbor are visible. This house, the Morris-Jumel Mansion, is the oldest remaining home in all of Manhattan. And while the city has grown considerably from 1765 (the year the house was built), meaning the house is no longer 11 miles from town and no longer has unobstructed views of New Jersey, Connecticut, or the New York Harbor, it is not hard to imagine that you are stepping into the 18th and 19th centuries when you walk into the Morris-Jumel Mansion.

The mansion has a very interesting history and offers great potential as a resource for a research paper. Built originally by the British Colonel Roger Morris for himself and his wife, Mary Philipse, it was abandoned when the Revolutionary War broke out (the Morrises were staunch loyalists). Having noticed the mansion's elevated position and grand view of the surrounding area, Washington used it as headquarters for the Continental Army from September 14 to October 21, 1776. From there, he planned the successful battle of Harlem Heights.

Although Washington never returned to the mansion during the war, after the British defeat he hosted a celebratory dinner there that was attended by a Revolutionary War Who's Who: John Adams, John Quincy Adams, Alexander Hamilton, Thomas Jefferson, and Aaron Burr. After the war, it was briefly a tavern before it returned to serving as a residence.

In 1810 Stephen Jumel purchased the mansion, and he and his wife, Eliza Bowen, lived in it until their deaths. After Stephen died, Eliza was briefly married to Aaron Burr. She divorced him, however, and returned to using Jumel's name. (She only used Burr's name during her travels in Europe because it increased her social status.)

Today most of the house is restored to the way it was when Eliza lived there. However, a few of the rooms and furnishings, including the dining room downstairs, reflect the period of the Morrises' residence. In addition, the bedroom Washington used is restored to how it would have looked as his headquarters, and one of the rooms upstairs is set up as Aaron Burr's office. The basement is restored to its original condition as kitchen and workroom and contains several original tools and replications.

This place is particularly strong in the early history of New York, daily life in early America, the Revolutionary War period, and the lives of George Washington, Aaron Burr, and the other inhabitants of the mansion. The archives include a volume of letters written by Washington while he was at the house and several letters by Burr. There's also a lot of information on early American architecture and furniture and ample information on the slaves and indentured servants who lived at the house. While other institutions often overlook slavery and indentured servitude, you can learn a lot about those who labored here from 1765 to 1865, representing two thirds of the inhabitants.

To gain access to the mansion's archives, which hold both books and personal documents of those who lived in the house, call the curator of the collections, Sheena Brown, at (212) 923-8008 to make an appointment. You should try and call a week in advance and have a general idea about what kind of information you are looking for. While use of the archives is free, you may have to pay ten cents a page for photocopies. Since you cannot copy all of the documents in the archives, be prepared to take a lot of notes. The archives are spotty and not good for very general historical topics but are very good in specific areas.

Don't be discouraged by the limited range of the documents. They reveal a great deal of information. Though this may not be the best place to start research, it's wonderful for case studies and finding specific examples of artifacts that you can discuss within a greater context. Even if you have done preliminary research, you should consider asking to see the eight-minute video about the mansion's history as well as the recently published book about the house, available in the archives and at the bookstore.

While visiting the mansion, keep in mind that you can find a lot of political history. Ask yourself what "equal" meant to all of the different people who lived there, and you might just find yourself with a paper topic. You might also consider how the changing people and décor reflect the changing identity of America. The architecture alone reveals how the new nation looked to Greece and Rome as models for its style and design as well as for its government. Also, ask the mansion staff about school programs. While they are not available to individual students, the information that the staff uses in the programs is available to you.

If the Morris-Jumel Mansion is at all related to what you are studying, we would definitely recommend visiting it.

Notes:

Address:	1230 Fifth Ave. at 104th St. New York, NY 10029
Telephone:	212.831.7272
Directions:	Take the 6 to E. 103rd St.
Hours:	Wednesday-Sunday 11:00am-5:00pm Closed Mondays & Tuesdays
Entry Fee:	$3 Students
Website:	www.elmuseo.org

El Museo del Barrio is a museum dedicated to "educating its diverse public in the richness of Caribbean and Latin American arts and cultural history." So, how can it help you do research on a U.S. history topic?

Well, **think about how many people in the U.S. have roots in Mexico or Puerto Rico, in Cuba or the Dominican Republic, in countries throughout South America. Think also about how much Latin culture has shaped U.S. culture: music, literature, language, food, dance.** And think about how much of the U.S. was part of Mexico before the Mexican War of 1846-48–that is, what's now California, Nevada, Utah, New Mexico, Arizona, and Texas–and how much those areas still reflect this heritage. **Whether your topic is cultural, political, or economic, there is much here that can be useful to you.** And if you are doing a paper on the exploration of North or South America or the colonization of North or South America or the history of the Native peoples of North or South America, this is the museum you should visit.

Did you know that people colonized the Caribbean long before Columbus arrived? They were nomads who lived in caves and temporary shelters, of Arawak descent (from the northern coast off what is now South America). In their search for food, they left the mainland, traveling in canoes out to the islands of the Caribbean. Their descendants evolved into the Taíno, the dominant culture in what later became Puerto Rico, Hispaniola, the Bahamas, and Jamaica.

In the exhibit, you learn about many aspects of Taíno culture and history–everything from their system of matrilineal descent (not patrilineal, like the system in the U.S. and Europe) to their astronomy to their use of symbols instead of an alphabet. You can study the cohoba ceremony, in which shamans mixed crushed shell and tobacco with cohoba to enhance what was already the strongest hallucinogen in the Americas. (Just don't study it too hard.) Or learn about the game the Taíno played on a central ceremonial court with a rubber ball—a precursor of modern-day volleyball. The game was so important that they even documented scores, and for all you supporters of women's sports out there, documents show teams made up entirely of women.

Studying the Taíno culture, especially in comparison to the European culture that devastated it, is fascinating. The Taíno heritage has shaped not just Latin American culture but North American culture as well. For example, their foods and even some of their words—"barbecue," "canoe," "hammock," "hurricane"—have made their way into both Spanish and English.

The exhibit on the Taíno is only half the museum. The other space features changing exhibits, and they are often a mix of art, history, politics, and culture. For example, past exhibits include "Pressing the Point: Parallel Expressions in the Graphic Arts of the Chicano and Puerto Rican Movements," which looked at prints and posters by artists who were politically active in the 1960's and 1970's. An exhibit on Juan Sanchez, a Brooklyn-born Puerto Rican artist and activist, used art to express Puerto Rican history and culture. Such exhibits will give you a lot of insight on the experiences and viewpoints of people in different Hispanic cultures.

In addition to the exhibits, El Museo does a lot to promote Latin American culture. **For students, it holds special hands-on workshops, guided gallery tours, and internships, in addition to classroom-oriented programs.** The museum also shows films (free), gives concerts, and hosts different cultural events in its theater. And it celebrates Latin American customs and holidays, such as Three Kings Day and Cinco de Mayo. The museum wants to teach you as well as share the holidays with you, so educational programs accompany events like the Three Kings Day community parade. If you are interested in participating in festivals, you should consider reserving a spot early because space is limited.

To find out more information, check out the museum's website.

Address:	28 Broadway New York, NY 10004
Telephone:	212.908.4519
Directions:	Take N or R to Rector St., 4 or 5 to Bowling Green, J or M to Broad St., 2 or 3 to Wall St.
Hours:	Tuesday-Saturday 10:00am-4:00pm Closed Mondays
Entry Fee:	$2 Adults (no student rate)
Website:	www.financialhistory.org

The Museum of American Financial History is a great museum to come visit for your research. However, unlike other museums with more wide-ranging holdings, this one will probably only help you if you're focused specifically on American financial history. And you should be aware that though the museum's exhibits are very interesting and detailed, there's only room to showcase one exhibit at a time, so check ahead to make sure the exhibit will be helpful for researching your topic.

When we went to the museum, we saw the exhibit "Born in New York: Wells Fargo – 150 Years of Entrepreneurial Spirit." It traced the history of Wells Fargo from 1852, when Henry Wells, William G. Fargo, and John Livingston started a business they called American Express, through the company's expansion to its current standing as one of the country's top businesses. The exhibit displays original and reproduced portraits, the *Wells Fargo Express* (the company put out a magazine from September 1912 to June 1918), tickets and receipts, furniture, machinery, commissions, models of the famous Concord Coach that carried much of Wells Fargo's overland traffic, and even quotations from individuals involved with the company's operations.

Though the exhibits change frequently, they tend to include certain features: paper documents, text, interactive parts, and a videotape that replays itself every couple minutes.

The Wells Fargo exhibit included tiles with questions for you to quiz yourself about the period, to help provide context. We found out who was president (Franklin Pierce), how many people lived in New York City (515,547), how much a cup of coffee in New York cost then

($0.04), and what the tallest building in the city was (Trinity Church). The exhibit also lets you use a telegraph, giving you a code for the alphabet and for some specific terms that Wells Fargo transmitted over the wire as part of its daily business.

Regardless of when you visit the museum, a small part of the room shows money.cnn.com and the accompanying T.V. channel. But a more interesting part of the exhibit space is a section of tickertape from the opening of the stock market on the fateful day of October 29, 1929, when the stock market crashed and the Great Depression is considered to have begun. In front of the tape, which is hung on the wall, is a real ticker tape machine that still works and will print out a message to you for free if you register in the museum's guest list.

The museum organizes events in conjunction with the exhibit on display. For the most up-to-date information on events and to find out if they require a reservation or fee, check the museum's website. The museum recommends that if you are interested in finance, particularly the stock market, you play the stock market game. For information on it, go to the Security Industry Association's website, *www.sia.com*. *New York Newsday* runs a similar program.

The best feature of the museum is its archives, which the museum allows you to use. You should call first to make an appointment and to find out what is required before you come in. They'll ask for a letter of recommendation from your school or teacher and an ID. You should have a specific research topic in mind when you call, and tell the staff in advance so they have time to find relevant documents before they meet with you. You'll need either to bring a disk, pay for a disk there, or pay for photocopying. These costs should be minimal, however.

Much of the information in the exhibits comes from the museum's archives, so if you are stuck for a topic you should consider starting with a list of old exhibits, which you can find online. At the moment, the museum is putting its archives online. Check the online archives before you call the museum to do research, to save yourself and the museum staff from duplicating information that is already accessible to you.

Also, be aware that the museum puts out a quarterly magazine. Articles from it are catalogued at the museum's website. If an article looks interesting, you can call and ask them to send you a hard copy. (Just remember you might have to cough up some change to cover the photocopy fee.) Realize that even though you might have to pay for it, it will at least be cheaper and easier than trying to find and buy the entire magazine. And be grateful that the museum is so accommodating, especially since it is very small and staff members always have their hands full. Although you should not be discouraged from calling the museum, keep in mind that the process of changing exhibits pretty much occupies the entire staff for the block of time it takes to install the new exhibit. So if you call while the museum is changing its exhibits, you should be a little extra patient if the staff doesn't get back to you right away.

Notes:

Museum of Chinese in the Americas

Address:	70 Mulberry St., 2nd floor New York, NY 10013
Telephone:	212.619.4785
Directions:	Take the N, R, W, Q, J, M, or 6 to Canal St.
Hours:	Tuesday-Sunday 12:00pm-5:00pm Closed Mondays
Entry Fee:	$1 Students
Website:	www.moca-nyc.org

Ever wonder what it would be like to step inside a Chinese lantern? That's what architect Billie Tsien was thinking when she designed the exhibit space for this museum's permanent exhibit, "Where is Home?" **It examines the lives of Chinese in the Americas, focusing on their transition from China to the United States and their struggle to find a place for themselves between the culture they leave behind and the one they find here.** The exhibit includes artifacts that immigrants brought with them from mainland China, Taiwan, and from stops on their way to the United States, as well as objects documenting their everyday life in America.

Not much text accompanies each individual piece. But together, the artifacts tell an amazing story about Chinese immigrants and their descendants as they search for a new identity that includes both Chinese and American cultures. Their stories show you history from the bottom up rather than from the top down. Here the history you learn in school and in books comes alive through the individuals who lived it. The exhibit also offers an interesting feature: visitors' responses to the question "Where Is Home?"

Another part of the exhibit features pictures taken by young Chinese Americans. Though this slide show demonstrates that the museum is contemporary and that the issues in the exhibit continue to be relevant, it probably won't help with your research. Teenagers smoking and sitting on a couch and several close-ups of the inside of a fridge come to mind. If you have been to high school, or even if you just know what it is to be a teenager, there is nothing in this slide show that you would need to come to the museum to find. Though it's only a few minutes long, your time at the museum could be much better spent.

Though the gallery is small and concentrates on the history of

Chinese people in New York, it offers great variety. Walk inside the lantern and find, for example, the story of Mrs. Chu Fat and the embroidered silk slippers she made for herself but didn't wear once she came to the U.S. You'll see a *chun kahm* (a four-string guitar), a picture of a 1924 semipro Chinese baseball team, Cantonese opera headdresses, advertising type cuts with both English letters and Chinese symbols, letters from a wife to her husband while he was fighting for the United States in World War II, and a business license from the City of New York.

There is even a ten-cent Chinatown newspaper from 1971 with headlines that read "Red China Enters UN," "Pat May Crowned NY 'Miss Chinatown," and "1950 Concentration Security Act Repealed" (the act that justified internment of minorities). Other objects include pictures of a Chinatown in Cuba and perhaps the most poignant piece in the exhibit, a series of photos that have been cut and pasted together to produce a complete family portrait. Most likely the family members could not all get together as the creator of the collage probably wished.

The permanent exhibit includes two special sections. One explores the Chinese American women's movement and the Civil Rights movement. The other tells the history of the Chun Kong Chow merchant family, which ran stores in Hong Kong and Melbourne in addition to the one they ran in New York City after the family came to the U.S. in 1926. They were one of the few families to immigrate after the 1882 Chinese Exclusion Act, which forbade Chinese men to bring their families with them to the United States unless the men were merchants. (Did you know this act wasn't scratched until 1943? But even afterward, strict quotas greatly limited the number of Chinese immigrants granted permission to enter the United States until the 1960s.)

A wonderful research tool available to you at the museum is the CD-ROM called "Transitions: The Changing Profile of New York Chinatown." It chronicles the development of Manhattan's Chinatown from the time the land was home to Werpoes Hill, a Native American village, to the present. The history is extensive. The CD-ROM traces all of the immigrant groups that have lived in what is now Chinatown, even those who inhabited the area before the arrival of Chinese immigrants and those groups who later lived alongside the Chinese.

The museum staff is very knowledgeable and helpful, supplying much additional information. Don't be afraid to ask questions. In fact, ask questions even if you think they may not be necessary. You never know what kind of wonderfully unexpected answer you might get.

The museum also hosts a whole variety of school programs, including workshops, lectures and even tours of Chinatown. For the most current information on programs, check the museum's website. Though it mentions that the museum has an extensive archive, the archive was closed for the 2002-2003 school year for reorganization.

Though this museum is relatively small and relatively new, if you are doing a project on **anything related to the history of the Chinese in the Americas, race relations, immigration, discrimination, or the history of New York City, the history of any ethnic group in New York City—including Native Americans, African Americans, Jews, Eastern Europeans, the Irish, or Germans—definitely stop at the museum.** MoCA has a lot to offer you.

There is a very reasonable suggested donation of $1 for students.

Notes:

Address:	1220 Fifth Ave. New York, NY 10029
Telephone:	212.534.1672
Directions:	Take the 6 to E. 103rd St.
	Take the 2 or 3 to W. 111th St.
Hours:	Wednesday-Saturday 10:00am-5:00pm
	Sundays 12:00pm-5:00pm
	Closed Mondays
	Tuesdays: Groups only
Entry Fee:	$4 Students
Website:	www.mcny.org

Wow. The Museum of the City of New York is fun to visit, no matter what you're interested in. This place rules. From giant flower lamps à la *Alice in Wonderland* to paintings of New York City people and places (old and recent), to a miniature scene of South Street in 1855, to entire rooms from different eras, to the red Thai silk embroidered ball gown from the Broadway musical *The King and I*, to the "Americas Six" fire engine from 1851. You name it, you'll find it here. This place has all sorts of interesting artifacts from all eras of New York City history.

Though the museum concentrates on New York City history, almost everything you find here can be applied to a broader, national historical context. The costumes and textiles, decorative arts, paintings and sculpture, prints and photographs, theater, and toys will astound you. To get an idea of the many different artifacts the museum owns, go online and check out the information on the collections.

Seek and you never know what sort of interesting ideas you shall find. For example, looking at the Astor Place Riot and theater exhibits can be a fascinating way to learn about the history of social class. Reading about the history of theater in New York, you learn about the city's first folk hero, "Mose," a character from the popular play *A Glance at New York*, who was based on a real New Yorker, a volunteer fireman and local tough guy from the Bowery named Moses. Legend surrounds this man, who is said to have been able to leap the East River and uproot a lamppost with one hand. It seems that Johnny Appleseed had a little competition.

Or visit "The Lubavitch of Brooklyn," an exhibit on the history and culture of a group of Hasidic Jews.

Lining the walls in the second floor hallway is a series of paintings of New York City called "Painting the Town." Included is an 1895 scene of Washington Square Park. Although the other paintings on display change, almost every era of the city seemed to be represented, so you could probably use them to study how New York's neighborhoods have been transformed over the years.

Of particular note is the museum's assortment of furniture. The second and fifth floors display rooms that are typical of the middle and upper classes of almost every period. A series of drawing rooms, bedrooms, and other restored interiors dating from 1740 to 1880 can be found intact, and John D. Rockefeller's bedroom and drawing room are exactly as they looked when he used them. You almost feel as if, by walking into the room, you are stepping into his life.

If you're interested in New York as a seaport, you should check out the exhibit on South Street on the second floor. There is a miniature model of South Street and a full-size representation of Robert Fulton leaning on the *Nassau*, a boat he designed that was the first steamboat on the Fulton Street Ferry Line.

Also, if you've ever collected dollhouses, note that the museum has a whole room of them. In addition, there are several different types of children's books and games. Some of the games will look familiar, but most are quite old and quite interesting. Perhaps you could use these exhibits to study education and how individuals, particularly children, spent their time in different eras.

Lastly, a mural, "Growing Up in NYC" by Robert Burghard, follows an East Side man's life between 1926 and 1944 and includes his impressions of the historical events of the period. It is a clever and touching work of art, one of the best that the museum displays.

One thing you should definitely do is check out the museum's calendar for information on workshops, lectures, films, and performances. Usually the programs are related to the current exhibits. If you have any questions, contact Robert Forloney, who works in the museum's Learning Department, at ext. 250.

Whether you are a history buff or you just want to get some help with your project, you might consider participating in New York City History Day. What you do is pick a historical topic and put together a primary-source history project that you enter in a

competition with other New York City high school kids. You can write a history paper, create your own museum exhibit, do a documentary, or put on an original performance. If you decide to do a traditional history paper, you have to do the project by yourself. Otherwise, you can work in a group of up to five people.

The New York City History Day winners go on to the New York State competition at Cooperstown. Winners there continue to the national competition. Contact Robert Forloney at ext. 250 for information. You will need a teacher to advise you, and your teacher will have to attend a workshop run by the museum.

Research opportunities may be available to you, depending on what you are studying. To find out if the Collections Access Department can help you, call at least a week ahead of when you would like to do your research, and have a pretty specific topic in mind. The amount of time it takes you to get an appointment will depend on which curatorial department you're looking into.

For students, there is a fee of $10.00 for a 2 1/2-hour-long appointment. Make sure that you have done a good deal of research in a library before you ask to do research here. Unless the information you are looking for is very specific to the museum, the Collections Access Department may suggest you start elsewhere.

Notes:

Museum of Modern Art QNS

Address:	33rd St. at Queens Blvd. Long Island City, Queens
Telephone:	212.708.9400
Directions:	Take the 7 local to 33rd St.
Hours:	Saturday-Monday & Thursday 10:00am-5:00pm Fridays 10:00am-7:45pm Closed Tuesdays & Wednesdays
Entry Fee:	$8.50 Students Friday 4:00pm-7:45pm Pay what you wish
Website:	www.moma.org

You might think that a modern art museum may give you trouble—not just because it offers art instead of documenting events, but because you're looking to do research about the past at an institution that specializes in the present. So where does that leave you? Somewhere in the recent past?

Well, don't let the word "modern" trick you: it describes an era, approximately the last one hundred years of art. So while you may find artwork here that is about as old as you are, you'll also find artwork here that dates back to the late 1800s. Modern shouldn't mean "don't do research here."

The Museum of Modern Art's (MoMA) collections are unbelievable. Its photography collection includes 25,000 works dating from 1840 to the present. And although it includes pictures taken solely for the sake of art, it also includes those taken by journalists, scientists, entrepreneurs, and even amateurs. **If you are studying a specific event that took place in the last hundred years, it might be valuable to you to see not just how an event was captured on film, but how different people from different backgrounds chose to examine the same event.** Just looking at one photograph, "Back" (1938) by Dorothea Lange (which you can find online at the museum's website), you could launch a discussion on the life of farmers during the Great Depression and how, as shown in the photograph, they had a great deal of time to talk and socialize, in part to keep up morale because even at harvest time there was not much work for them to do. You never know how a picture can give a new dimension, especially a human dimension, to a paper that can easily get lost in dryness and facts.

The photography collection is not the only place where you can find photographs. They're also in the museum's architecture and design collection, together with drawings and models. The museum also has design and graphic design collections, with more than 7,000 objects, from posters and typography to cars and tableware.

There is also a film collection covering the entire film-making era and all genres—everything from films to stills to videos. You can go from Michael Snow's *Wavelength* (1967) to original negatives from the Edison company.

The painting and sculpture collection covers every major artist and art movement in the past 100 years. It holds over 3,000 artworks, with pieces by such masters as Van Gogh, Picasso, Matisse, and Cezanne. And the prints and illustrated books collection has almost 40,000 items.

Unfortunately, now that we've described the amazing collections that MoMA owns, we have the unfortunate task of informing you that the majority of these items will be inaccessible to you—at the very least, while MoMA is still in Queens and its Manhattan home is undergoing renovation. So why did we mention all that stuff? To give you an idea of just some of the amazing exhibits MoMA can put together for you, with even more in the future. Though the space MoMA has at Queens is limited, its exhibits reflect the breadth and amazing quality of the collections. While some exhibits will more easily lend themselves to a history paper than others, you should take the time to walk through all of the exhibits because you never know what kind of painting, what kind of artist, or what kind of period will be represented and how it might be interesting to use in your paper.

No matter when you visit the museum, you should walk through the one ongoing exhibit, "To Be Looked At: Painting and Sculpture from the Collection." At least a third, if not almost half is comprised of works by American artists such as Jasper Johns, Chuck Close, Roy Lichtenstein, Ellsworth Kelly, Agnes Martin, Andy Warhol, Robert Rauschenberg, and Marcel Duchamp. Look at Andy Warhol's interpretation of Campbell's soup cans firsthand. **You would be surprised how much art can reflect aspects of American culture that could be explored from a historical perspective.** What does Rauschenberg's 1955 *Bed* tell us about how Americans defined a bed and the kind of associations and values they placed on it?

Typically, the museum has two types of exhibits: those focused on only one type of item or idea vs. very broad ones that incorporate a lot of different items or ideas under the umbrella of a common theme. When we visited the museum, it had two very specific exhibits and a broad, theme-based one.

The first two special exhibits we looked at were specific. One was about cars, the other about Astoria through photographs taken by Rudy Burckhardt. Okay, cars sound cool. But what historical research could you do by looking at them? Well, you don't have to be writing about cars for this exhibit to be useful to you. Ask yourself why a certain type of car was made and how that reflects history. How does a Utility 2 Ton 4x4 M38A1 Truck (i.e., a Jeep) differ from a Volkswagen Type I Sedan (i.e., a Beetle)? Who were the cars originally designed for? Who eventually drove them? Where were they driven? Why?

The second exhibit we saw was "A Walk through Astoria and Other Places In Queens: Photographs by Rudy Burckhardt." It showcases works from two of Burckhardt's private albums, accompanied by five sonnets by Edwin Derby that are also about walking around in Astoria. **This exhibit captures snapshots of both people and places, including pictures of children, families, gas stations, empty lots, and buildings. If you're studying the 1940's, New York, or better yet, Queens, specifically Astoria, then this would be a great find for you and your paper.**

The exhibit "Trans-Histories" could be very applicable to a paper topic. You're probably asking yourself what a trans-history is. Well, this exhibit examines how labor and leisure have been affected by the African diaspora. Topics include the legacy of slavery, the coverage of war in Afghanistan, and the economy of Third World countries. One piece in particular, a film by Fatimah Tuggar, *Meditation on Vacation 2002*, explores the effects of globalization that make it fun and easy for American tourists to vacation in poor Caribbean nations while at the same time making it very difficult for people living there to save enough money to travel, or even live well enough to be able to take any sort of vacation or rest. While art serves as a medium for Tuggar's comments, her comments are by no means restricted to art.

Consider viewing "Ansel Adams," which will exhibit 114 of the photographer/conservationist's finest prints. They capture the natural wonder that is Yosemite and so much of the West. If you are writing about manifest destiny or the environment, studying Adams and his work could lead to an interesting component of your paper.

In terms of doing research at MoMA, your best bet is probably the museum's website combined with the public library. While the museum has a library, archives, and several study centers, the library and archives are not meant for high school students and the study centers are closed indefinitely, or at least closed while MoMA is renovating and expanding its site in Manhattan. However, **the website has a series of frequently asked questions about doing research and suggests how to go about researching outside of the museum.** You can search the contents of the library, archives, and study centers online, using the database (available through the website).

One thing you should definitely check on the website is its links to MoMA Learning and to Programs and Events. While as an individual you cannot join in the museum's school class programs, you can take advantage of its adult and public programs. You can find programs on almost anything, and they provide you with a useful context in which to view some of the artwork on display. In just the month of October, the museum held programs on Latin American architecture from the 1930s to the 1960s, how New York and Parisian artists responded to the conflicts of World War II (including capitalism, socialism, and communism), American veterans who used the G.I. bill to study art in Paris after World War II, art design from the Atomic Age, Rudy Burckhardt's photographs of Queens, fifteen new billboards in Chelsea and Long Island City, and contemporary architects.

Some of the public events are even aimed specifically at you, the high schooler visiting without a class, and they're free. **Friday nights from 5 to 8 p.m., MoMA invites you to sit for a screening of classic, foreign, and current movies, to talk with museum educators about them, and to chow down on free pizza and soda. It doesn't get much better than this.** Themes for the movies have included teens taking on the world and what it means to be an immigrant. *Rushmore, The 400 Blows, Boyz N the Hood, Liberty Heights, La Ciudad*, and *Coming to America* were all films screened in the fall of 2002. (If you really like the film program, you should consider checking out the museum's film and media exhibits at the Gramercy Theatre on 23rd Street in Manhattan.)

If you are more interested in exploring exhibits, you should consider the after-hours program. On designated Thursday afternoons (4 to 5 p.m.), museum educators will meet with you and other high school students to discuss current exhibits. You should be aware that many programs take place offsite, either in Manhattan or at the Queens Public Library. Also, when you visit the museum you should ask for a list of gallery talks, tours, and other events to take place there that day. MoMA is one of the few museums that makes itself very accessible to individual high school kids doing research on their own and on their own time. You should definitely take advantage of this!

Notes:

Museum of Television and Radio

Address:	45 West 53rd St. New York, NY 10019
Telephone:	212.621.6800
Directions:	Take the E or V to Fifth Ave./53rd St.
Hours:	Tuesday-Sunday 12:00pm-6:00pm Thursdays 12:00pm-8:00pm Fridays 12:00pm-9:00pm (theaters only) Closed Mondays
Entry Fee:	$8 Students $5 Students under 14
Website:	www.mtr.org

Where can you go to see footage of Vietnam, the Civil Rights Movement, Leonard Bernstein and the New York Philharmonic, classic SNL's dating back to the 1970s, the 1968 Academy Awards, the Negro baseball league, and Andy Warhol? And where can you go to listen to old radio spots of Winston Churchill, Babe Ruth and even old radio commercials for Chun King Chop Suey or Bayer, and still have time to get your fix of your favorite TV show?

Come visit the Museum of Television and Radio. This is a place where it's fun to study anything. Don't think it has to be strictly media-related. **If it's been on TV or on the radio, they've got it. Since practically everything that is relevant to American history has been addressed by TV and radio programs, you can come here to study (yes) practically anything.**

This is not a typical museum. It does not have typical exhibits. Say goodbye to sore feet and hello to comfortable chairs. Though there is one small room on the first floor where, in typical museum-visitor fashion, you walk around to view objects displayed on walls and screens, this is the only such room. The main exhibits exist as a series of narrated film clippings on a specific theme that run in different theaters in the building at different times during the day.

Besides the exhibits, the museum also runs several shows from its archives on the big screen. In the late summer of 2002, the screenings for the day included: *The Curse of Mr. Bean*, *The Muppet Show/Liberace*, *Jerry Seinfeld's Stand-Up Confidential*, *Batman: The Purr-fect Crime/Better Luck Next Time*, *David Bowie: Sound and*

Vision, Strangers with Candy (unaired pilot), *The Mary Tyler Moore Show* (the first and last episodes), *The Practice: Pilot, The Great Stand-Ups: 60 Years of Laughter, Super Bowl: Super Showcase for Commercials, Before the Ball: The Unseen Cinderella Rehearsal Tape, Science Fiction: a Journey into the Unknown, Heat Vision and Jack* (unaired pilot), and *Sid Caesar Highlights.* In the Radio Listening Room, five programs were playing all day: *Rare Voices of the Twentieth Century, The Radio Interview, David Bowie: Hazy Comic Jive, Take Me Out to the Ball Game*, and *Rock 'n' Roll Radio.*

The museum has a library where you can look up and view almost anything (i.e., refer to first paragraph). Access is free with admission. When you enter the museum, you should make an appointment in the library. When your appointment time arrives, make your way up to the fourth floor. You'll be seated at a computer, where you can search the museum's holdings either by looking at highlights of the collection, the collection itself, or the archives.

Once you've chosen where you want to look, you choose what you want to look at: T.V., radio, or advertising. If you know what you are searching for, you can type in specific words and see what the computer comes up with for you—e.g., themes, titles, actors. When you click an individual program, the computer will list basic information about it as well as a detailed paragraph or two, so that you can decide if it interests you.

Once you have chosen programs, a list of your selections will print out and you will wait about 5 to 15 minutes for the library staff to gather your tapes. **Then you go downstairs (you never hold tapes) to the viewing/listening room, where you can have a seat at a small cubicle with a T.V. You can play both videos and tapes of radio programs here, and you have the option of rewinding and fast-forwarding.** There is a two-hour maximum limit on the viewing/listening room, but if the room isn't full, the limit isn't enforced.

Be aware that if you choose to search in the archives as opposed to the on-site collection, you might have to wait as long as a week to view your selections. The only delay you might experience with the collection would occur if a curator was using the tape you want to watch. The likelihood of this is slim, however. If you want to know if specific shows are available, you might consider calling ahead and asking a librarian, but don't call and ask the library staff to check a zillion things for you. If you plan on spending a lot of time searching or if you're not sure what you're looking for, you should come and search for yourself.

The museum offers several educational resources to you, the student. Typically, a museum educator works with a teacher by leading classes in the morning. These classes, about 90 minutes long, are media-based and examine specific themes. For example, one of them discusses the Cold War: how it was portrayed on T.V. and how T.V.'s portrayal shaped the Cold War—particularly how it helped create hysteria. In the class, you could expect to see and discuss news coverage of the Cold War, public service announcements, and clips from documentaries and science fiction films. Other classes focus on documentary filmmaking, advertising and persuasion, the Civil Rights Movement, New York City, political advertising, violence, and women.

Although these classes are not intended for individual students, the museum educators may be willing to let you sit in and take notes. You should call first to find out what kind of classes are being offered and ask if you could sit in on a particular one because you think it might help with your paper. If you are invited to do so, be sure you can prove that you don't have school on that day or that you have permission to miss it. A note from a teacher or principal on school stationery should do it, but you might want to double-check.

Probably more realistically accessible to you are the museum's videographies. Put together with education in mind, each one is a series of clips that focus on a particular topic. Just some of the topics include technology, immigrants, jazz, the Cold War, civil rights, and the changing roles of women. **The museum has even put together videographies to help you study for the essay questions on your Regents exams.** They've already got review material for the Global Regents exam and are currently collecting review material for the American History exam. You use the worksheets and a videography to practice writing essay questions from real exams. Even if you are not reviewing for the Regents yet, these could be really good sources of information for you.

Be warned: there is a lot of film in one videography. One sample essay on human rights (a review for Global) includes seven different programs that each range from 30 to 90 minutes in length. You may want to set aside an entire day if you don't plan to make multiple visits to the museum. By the end of the 2002-2003 school year, an index of videographies should be available in the library. Until then, you should contact the education department to find out which ones could be helpful to you.

The museum educators may also recommend that you watch footage of different historic events and documentaries about these events, both of which the museum has on tape. To give you an idea, the museum has the following events on tape: "Lindbergh's Arrival and Speech in Washington (1927)," "Franklin D. Roosevelt's First Inaugural Address (1933)," "The *Hindenburg* Disaster (1937)," "Hitler's Address to the Reichstag (1939)," "Pearl Harbor Bulletin (1941)," "Buchenwald: Edward R. Murrow's First-hand Account (1945)," "Army-McCarthy Hearings (1954)," "See It Now: Report on Senator Joseph McCarthy (1954)," "The Cuban Missile Crisis (1962)," "The March on Washington (1963)," "The Zapruder Film of the John F. Kennedy Assassination (1963)," "The Kennedy State Funeral (1963)," "President Johnson's Address on Vietnam (1967)," "The Assassination of Dr. Martin Luther King Jr. (1968)," "The Robert Kennedy Assassination (1968)," "The Democratic National Convention in Chicago (1968)," "The Journey of *Apollo 11*: Moonwalk (1969)," "The House Judiciary Impeachment Committee (1974)," "President Nixon's Resignation (1974)," "President Reagan's Inauguration and Freeing the American Hostages in Iran (1981)," "The Shuttle Explosion (1986)," "Iran-Contra (1987)," "The Fall of the Berlin Wall (1989)," "The Rodney King Videotape (1991)," and "The Persian Gulf War (1991)."

The museum also has two-part to twenty-six-part miniseries documenting such topics as the history of the United States, intellectual history, Western art and architecture, New York, immigrants, Henry Ford, the Great Depression, World War II, the Cold War, the Civil Rights Movement, Vietnam, computers, and the 20th century in America.

There are also lectures and seminars on a wide range of topics: for example, the relationship between the media and the military from World War II through the Gulf War, how African Americans are depicted on television, and most recently, how international press coverage and U.S. press coverage of 9/11 have differed. The museum has tapes of all its lectures and seminars, which you can watch there. If you are interested in attending a seminar or lecture, you should contact the education department, which may be able to offer you a complimentary ticket.

One thing you do not want to overlook is the museum's radio recordings. You can listen to anything from Winston Churchill's speeches to all Roosevelt's fireside chats to *The Shadow*, *Superman*, and several other radio dramas. Although the following is probably not going to help you at all with your research, it's worth a mention: if you can get together a group of about 25 students and 120 bucks among you, you can record an old radio drama script or one that you've written. You get to do everything from characters' voices to sound effects.

For questions regarding videographies, documentaries, lectures, seminars, classes, or any other special programs, contact Claire Riccardi, Coordinator for High School Programs at (212) 621-6724 or criccardi@mtr.org. For general museum questions, call the front desk at (212) 621-6600.

Notes:

Notes:

National Museum of the American Indian

Address:	One Bowling Green New York, NY 10004
Telephone:	212.514.3700
Directions:	Take the 4 or 5 to Bowling Green
Hours:	Daily 10:00am-5:00pm
	Thursdays 10:00am-8:00pm
Entry Fee:	Free
Website:	www.nmai.si.edu

A story to start with: where did Wall Street get its name? You may not expect to find out at the National Museum of the American Indian. But as you'll see when you read on, there's no place more appropriate to learn about the early history of Wall Street.

In 1626, Peter Minuit "bought" Manhattan for trade goods worth 60 guilders. Unfortunately, how the Native people of the island understood "bought" and how the Europeans did differed greatly. The Europeans believed they now had the exclusive right to live on the land. The Native people believed that the land could not exclusively belong to anyone, any more than water or sunlight could. They thought that the Europeans were making a gift to thank them for sharing the land. As relations turned sour, the Europeans built a wall to keep the Natives out. Where was it? Ironically, not far from where the National Museum of the American Indian stands, on what today we know as Wall Street.

Native American. American Indian. First Nation's People. They all describe the many groups of indigenous people who were the first inhabitants of North and South America. With a visit here you can expand your knowledge of their crucial part of American history, including your knowledge of the perspectives of many different Native American groups on American history. And since it's a Smithsonian Museum, it's free to the public.

The museum is fascinating. Just the building itself, located in the George Gustav Heye Center at the Alexander Hamilton Custom House, starts you off with an irony. As you approach it, look for a large sculpture of a female figure representing the U. S., which is crushing the famed Aztec city Quetzalcoatl. Behind it is a Native person surrounded by broken Native artifacts. The scene is meant to triumphantly depict the United States conquering and destroying the Native American way of life. But it decorates a building that now pays tribute to American Indian cultures that continue to endure.

Between the building, the exhibits, the programs, and the library and research center, you could keep yourself busy for days, even weeks, at a time. Okay, so where to start? Visit the museum and look through its exhibits. There are two large exhibits and two smaller ones. They change frequently, so it's a good idea to check before you visit that the exhibit you want to see is actually at the New York City museum. (There are three National Museums of the American Indian, and it is very easy to look at the dates and descriptions of exhibits while overlooking their locations.)

The Native influence on New York was shown in a recent exhibit, "Booming Out: Mohawk Ironworkers Build New York." You may have seen one famous picture in the exhibit: the 1928 photograph by Lewis Hine of nine men sitting high up above the city on a huge beam, during a break from construction on what would be known as the Rockefeller Center. Three of the men were Mohawk. The Mohawk communities of the Akwesasne (northern New York and Canada) and the Kahnawake (near Montreal) have a huge presence in the ironworking industry, and the exhibit's pictures captured them as they helped to define the famous New York skyline. These guys worked on almost every city landmark in the last century. The Empire State Building, the George Washington Bridge, the United Nations buildings, and what was the World Trade Center are just a few of the magnificent structures that Mohawk ironworkers helped build.

Another recent exhibit, "Spirit Capture: Native Americans and the Photographic Image," reflected a basic theme of the museum: it asked visitors **to examine how American Indians have been portrayed throughout the history of the United States, and to learn a fuller and a more accurate history of the many different Native American peoples.** This mission is also seen in the goal of the museum's education department: to improve the teaching of Native American history in high schools.

The education department also runs all of the museum's public programs. There are three kinds or programs: expressive culture, workshops, and interpretive culture. The expressive culture programs occur every day around 2:00 p.m. They do not require a reservation and are free. These can be anything from a demonstration of Native American artwork to Native American celebrations. You should find out what the expressive culture activity will be on the day of your visit. The workshops and the interpretive culture programs require reservations and may require a fee. Arts and crafts workshops often require a materials fee. Examples of workshops include ancient Mayan backstrap loom weaving, making Iroquois raised beadwork, and a group making an outfit for an Iroquois couple. For information on workshops call (212) 514-3714.

The interpretive culture programs include walking tours of New York that focus on the Native history of Manhattan, and book festivals where prominent writers and story tellers read and discuss their work. The museum also screens films and videos. The series includes historical fiction and documentaries about the lives of different indigenous peoples of the Americas. When you come to the museum, ask for a calendar of events. Most of the information in the calendar of events is also available on the museum's website, www.nmai.si.edu/heye/index.html.

The best part about the museum for doing research is that it has a resource center that is geared specifically to you. It's free and does not require any reservation. If your topic is about Native Americans, then it's here. You just walk in, fill out a sheet about what kind of information you are looking for, and give it to the librarian.

Just some of the available reading material in the waiting area includes *Cobblestone*, the history magazine for young people; *Indian Country*, "The Nation's Leading American Indian Newspaper"; the *Pequot Times*; the *Choctaw Community News*; the *Sioux Messenger*; and the *Cherokee Advocate*. We came across a lot of interesting information, on topics such as the Navajo Code Talkers (a group of Navajos who spoke their native language as a code for the U.S. military during World War II; because of its complexities, the enemies were unable to break it) and how the 86,500-acre Nez Perce reservation in Iowa is only 30% of the land promised in the treaty that established the reservation in 1863.

The computer areas consist of four workstations that can each be viewed by up to three people. One computer station is just for Internet research. The other three are for using CD-ROMs. On the CD-ROMs you can learn about stuff like the original Native inhabitants of Manhattan, a Native jewelry maker, a beadworker from the Hunkpapa Lakota, and pow-wows. Did you know that (back in the days when taking a ferry to Staten Island wasn't free) wampum beads were used as currency by non-Natives and were accepted in the early 1900s as payment for the Staten Island ferry ride?

The material that the librarian will prepare for you could come in almost any form. Though the resource center mainly has books, it also contains videotapes and musical recordings. The museum also has "discovery boxes" of everyday life: hunting and fishing, pow-wows, weaving and textiles, and the buffalo. In each box are a series of artifacts for you to look at. To give you an idea: the box on the buffalo contains the tools that would have been made from that animal. You can examine the dung that would have been used as fuel, the bladder that would have been used to contain water, and hooves, carved horns, and bones. The boxes are accompanied by reading material that gives context.

The best way to use the resource center is to just come and explore. The only drawbacks are that it is a non-lending library (you can't take any material home) and that you can photocopy a maximum of twelve pages for free—so bring some change for the copier and/or a huge notepad to fill with a ton of notes. To contact the Resource Center, call (212) 514-3799 or e-mail nin@ic.si.edu. You can also get a lot of information about the museum's educational programs and about the Resource Center online at www.conexus.si.edu/main.htm.

Notes:

National Museum of the American Indian

New-York Historical Society

Address:	2 W. 77th St. New York, NY 10024
Telephone:	212.873.3400
Directions:	Take the B, C to 81st St.
Hours:	Tuesday-Sunday 10:00am-5:00pm Closed Mondays
Entry Fee:	$4 Students
Website:	www.nyhistory.org

So you want to go the New-York Historical Society? Well, maybe not, but really, you should. Why? Because you want a good grade on the paper you're writing, and going to this museum is going to be an enormous help in achieving that goal. We didn't know this place even existed when we were sent there for this guidebook, but once we arrived we were blown away. While there are only three floors of museum space, there is more information in those three floors than you can... (insert silly colloquialism here). **The New-York Historical Society has a wealth of resources for any subject on early American and New York history.**

Here are two exhibits that will give you an idea of the kind of things you can expect to find here. Of particular interest to us were an exhibit on the culture of New York City rooftops and one about visual interpretations of music. People do some insane things on their rooftops, and the New-York Historical Society had pictures! They grow gardens, have cookouts, and sleep (yeah, sleep...). The pictures about music ranged from portraits of musicians done with fingerprints to dancing notes to abstract interpretations of a piece of music (some of whose colors were as loud as the music that inspired them!). So, while this is hardly the most famous museum in the city, it is certainly one of the most interesting. Below is a more detailed description of the collection and how you can use it most effectively.

The New-York Historical Society has three main things to offer: the Luce Center on the top floor; the galleries on the ground floor, which houses exhibits both specific to New York and pertinent to the entire nation; and the library in between. The Henry Luce III Center for the Study of American Culture holds the Society's permanent collection of American artifacts. This newly constructed and visually pleasing space allows the museum new freedom in displaying a greater portion of its vast collection. It promotes "object-based" learning: that is to say, there is very little text accompanying the displays so that viewers may form their own opinions on the pieces that they see. While first impressions are useful, since you are coming here because, presumably, you are not yet an expert on the objects you will be viewing, you should consider using an "acoustiguide."

The items in the Luce Center are grouped into seven different categories: paintings, sculpture, furniture, decorative objects, tools for home and trade, Tiffany lamps, and the "Mezzanine" collection (small archaeological artifacts). The majority of this art is American, from the 1600s to the present. The sculpture collection includes portraits, death masks, still-life art, and even tombstones. In addition, there are over 500 pieces of furniture, including George Washington's inaugural armchair and Valley Forge bed and the desk on which Clement Clark Moore wrote "A Visit From Saint Nicholas."

The decorative arts collection contains more than 8,000 objects made from silver, ceramic, metal, pewter, and glass, dating from the 18th century to the present. They include everything from locally made stoneware to a 381-piece silver dinner service that Commodore Perry received for negotiating open trade with Japan. The "Tools for Home and Trade" section includes thousands of objects from homes, shops, and farms from the Dutch colonial period to the early 20th century. The Luce Center also has 132 beautiful Tiffany lamps on display, one of the best collections worldwide. Badges, medals, firefighting and police equipment, jewelry, military gear, weapons, souvenirs, textiles, needlework, toys, games, and dolls are just some of the many small objects in the Mezzanine collection.

Unique to the New-York Historical Society are some of its more bizarre and arcane collections. You may have collected something like bottle caps, baseball cards, dolls, or stickers. Well, some of the Society's collections—usually donated by some individuals with some very interesting interests (perhaps even obsessions)—consist only of different variations on one single and, probably in the annals of history museums, usually overlooked, item—like apple peelers. But other collections such as display buttons (think politics and advertising) may be of more use to you.

So what else besides apple peelers and campaign buttons can you expect to see? Well, how do cartoons, examinations of a well-known character from an important historical novel, the history of women in the workplace, rare maps, and kids' games sound?

One 2003 exhibit: "The Games We Played: Victorian Games from the Liman Collection." Using kids' games for my research project in American history? Sounds almost too good to be true, but kids' games are made by adults, and you'd be surprised at how much they tend to reflect the political thought of the period in which they were made. One thing is for sure: many of these games were anything but innocent. Examples from the Civil War era were often unabashedly racist, such as "Jim Crow Ten Pins."

Also, you may not think that war games are that unusual for kids to play—after all, we've all probably come into contact with a GI Joe at some point in our formative years. However, we're not talking fake punches and pows with exclamations such as "Take that, you evil blah-blah-blah!" We're talking maps and countries here—full-out strategized global war. In these games, the spirit of imperialism isn't too hard to find. In "Mimic War," for example, the player wins the game by taking over the most foreign nations. The values of the Industrial Revolution and Gilded Age show through in this exhibit, and it is interesting to see how certain societal trends are present in even the most basic forms of entertainment.

"Enterprising Women: 250 Years of American Business" is another 2003 exhibit. It will be of interest to you for almost every topic. The contributions women make to the economy, World War II, women's rights, labor laws, family life—really, this exhibit supports any topic having to do with the role of women in society and how that role has changed. Lastly, a show on the New York cartoonist Jules Feiffer, whose satirical drawings influenced politics years ago, runs from February to June. If you are studying anything that bridges politics and art, you should consider visiting this exhibit.

The Society is currently working on a complete database of information on all of the objects on display. While many items are already catalogued, soon you will be able to research most of the objects you see on the computers in the Luce Center. The library is meant to be used by scholars, however, so as a high school student, you will need a really compelling reason for requesting access to primary sources and other library materials. This library is not where you would start your research, or even where you would do the bulk of it. You would only be considered for access to the library if you couldn't find what you want anywhere else.

If you do use the library, you can see Lincoln's Civil War letters, Washington's military plans from 1781, and a fine collection of pre-1820 newspapers. One of sixteen members of the Independent Research

Library Association, the library is non-circulating and its stacks are closed, but its contents can be searched online using NYU's "Bobcat" system. Even if you're not granted access to the library, you should still look up its contents online through Bobcat to find out if there are any documents that you could use in your paper. You can request that photocopies of original documents be sent to you by mail.

To find out about programs aimed at high school students, call Rachel Schreck, Coordinator of Middle and High School Programs, at (212) 873-3400 ext. 276. She is very knowledgeable and will be happy to help you. You should also contact her for information regarding the library, rather than calling the main number.

Notes:

New-York Historical Society

Website:	www.nypl.org
Telephone:	Check the website for specific locations, hours, phone

One stop for anyone writing or researching anything should be a library, and what better library could you ask to have at your fingertips than the New York Public Library (NYPL)? It has more than just one location. It's a huge network of buildings and people that extends throughout the city and includes branch libraries and research libraries.

Branch libraries allow you to take out books. If you want, though, there is ample space for you to read and work. To take books out, you do need a library card, but getting one is very easy: you just have to show proof that you are a resident of New York State. You can do so with an ID card or an envelope with your name and address on it that has been mailed to you (postmarked). **The branch libraries tend to be smaller and much more localized, sometimes specializing in certain departments. Many of their holdings reflect the people who use them most frequently, usually those who live in the surrounding neighborhoods.**

For example, if you are looking for foreign texts, particularly German, Russian, and Chinese, you should try the branch libraries on the Lower East Side. So, depending on what you are researching, you may want to travel to a branch outside of your neighborhood. You can search the branch libraries from any Internet source, including computers at your own local library, through LEO on the NYPL's home page. LEO is the catalog for all 85 NYPL branch libraries located in the Bronx, Manhattan, and Staten Island. If you find a book you like, be careful to check whether you can take it out or not. Branch libraries do have small sections of books for reference only that you cannot check out.

The research libraries are much larger than the branch libraries, but there are fewer of them. Located throughout the city, they do not require a library card because they do not allow you to check out books. Instead, you can look up a book and then ask the librarian to bring it to you. You must stay in the reading room area (where there are tables and computers and ample room to work comfortably) and return the book before you leave. There are four NYPL research libraries, and each one is specialized: the Humanities and Social

Sciences Library; the Science, Industry, and Business Library; the Schomburg Center for Research in Black Culture; and the New York Public Library for the Performing Arts. To search their holdings, use "CATNYP," which you can access from any Internet source by going to the NYPL's home page.

The New York Public Library, arguably the world's finest, provides you with more than just books. Several of its libraries, especially the research facilities, offer computers for you to access the catalogue, search online, and do word processing and even printing. A few of the libraries, including the Humanities and Social Sciences Research Library, even offer Internet connection if you bring a laptop along. WordPerfect 6.0, Lotus 1-2-3, Microsoft Office 97, ClarisWorks, and Print Shop Deluxe are all examples of the software that is available to you, free of charge. Not every branch has all of these programs, so you should check beforehand.

The libraries also have musical recordings, videos, magazines, newspaper, and microfilms. **Many of the research facilities' holdings even include primary documents that you can use to reconstruct the lives of ordinary people throughout American history.** You'll find such famous works of print as a Gutenberg Bible and Jefferson's manuscript copy of the Declaration of Independence. As the largest library system in the world, the NYPL also holds a large variety and quantity of literature.

The libraries also host many exhibits and activities. The research libraries in particular have very interesting exhibits and displays that are full of information and are free to the public. Though typically smaller, these displays rival those of any of the great museums you can find in the city. **All of the libraries, branch and research alike, sponsor many events, such as lectures, films, concerts, plays, writers' readings, story hours, tutoring, discussions, arts and crafts, and a variety of workshops.**

For specific information on any of the libraries –holdings, computers, exhibits, activities, hours, directions, etc.– visit the NYPL's website at www.nypl.org.

People travel from all over the country and the world to visit the New York Public Library, online and in person. For you, it is only a stone's throw away. USE IT and realize how lucky you are to be living in such a world-class city and have resources like this one right in your back yard.

Schomburg Center for Research in Black Culture

Address:	515 Malcolm X Blvd., New York, NY 10037
Telephone:	212.491.2200
Directions:	Take the 2 or 3 to W. 135th St.
Hours:	See Website
	Closed Sundays & Mondays
Website:	www.nypl.org/research/sc/sc.html

It's hard to think of a topic in American history that does not include African-American history. The Schomburg is a must for your list of research resources.

An amazing source of information (it is one of the four New York Public Library research libraries), this is not only a place where tons of great material is available (for free, remember). The information is also very accessible, and you will have help navigating the library's vast holdings.

When you enter, you will have to sign in and leave any large items at the bag/coat check. Make your way downstairs to the General Research and Reference Division, which will be your starting point no matter what kind of information you are looking for. In the two large rooms you will find desk space and computers with Internet access. (Be warned: the computers are for researching only, not word processing.) You should search the catalogue for books and artifacts that may be of interest to you.

You can ask a librarian for help. Once you know what you would like to look at, you fill out a small slip of paper with the item's call number and title, and the librarian will retrieve it for you. (Remember that this is a research library, not a branch library, so you cannot take books out with you—only look at them in the library.) You will also have access to microfilm and microfiche (which is what publications such as newspapers are stored on) and several 19th-century genealogy records.

Although most of the library's holdings are in English, and there is a very strong collection of items about the history of Harlem and of African Americans in New York City, you will also find items from South America, the Caribbean, and Sub-Saharan Africa. You

can find information from anywhere in the world about people of African descent, and you may be surprised to find out just how widespread the African heritage is. Among texts from both the U.S. and abroad, the library has works in several European languages and over 200 indigenous African and Creole tongues.

But getting back to American history: as you explore the General Research and Reference Division and the other four divisions (Art and Artifacts; Manuscripts, Archives, and Rare Books; Moving Image and Recorded Sound; and Photographs and Rare Prints), you will be able to find anything and everything. **Holdings range from documentaries to dramas, from advertisements to TV programs that discuss African-American concerns across the U.S., from recordings of traditional and contemporary music from several African-American cultures (including recordings of the blues, jazz, rhythm, and rap) to speeches from the Civil Rights Movement.** You can look at sheet music, scripts, playbills, broadsides, essays, short stories, poetry, articles, and personal letters and notes by famous leaders and scholars. There are photographs, sculptures, paintings, prints, illustrations, textiles, masks, instruments, weaponry, and artifacts—including some with great emotional resonance, such as slave shackles. The list goes on: coins, stamps, political buttons, quilts, uniforms, and clothing!

And that is by no means a complete summary. Though you can't start out at any of the other four divisions, you can be directed to them from General Research and Reference. To get a better idea of what the Schomburg has to offer you, go online and look through their website. Read about their different collections and look through the online exhibits, many of which came from past library exhibits. You can even look up books before you get to the library on CATNYP (the online catalogue of the New York Public Library, http://www.nypl.org/research/chss/grd/resguides/catnyp.html). Call the Research and General Reference Division at (212)491-2218 with any questions about getting started with your research. For general questions about the Schomburg Center, call the main switchboard at (212) 491-2200.

Just a few of the great areas for research papers you'll come across are: the Harlem Renaissance, the Works Progress Administration, the Black Arts Movement (1960s-1970s), black urban life, the Civil Rights Movement, the Niagara Movement and the NAACP, and important African-American historical figures, whether actors, musicians, authors, athletes, scholars, or political leaders.

The library offers programs and performances for the public (check online for a schedule), but of particular interest is the Junior Scholars Program, for students aged eleven to seventeen. It takes place from 10-3 on Saturdays from October to June, and if accepted you are expected to attend each session. You will learn about African-American culture and heritage through such activities as lectures, films, performances, and trips. Last year's participants produced their own magazine and video about their experiences in the program. Though free, the program is competitive and can fill up quickly. Applications are usually due by mid August, but if the program is under-enrolled they accept participants into September. Call (212) 491-2011 for information and an application.

The museum is part of the HSCC, the Harlem Strategic Cultural Collaborative. This group of organizations preserves Harlem's heritage and promotes the growth of culture in Harlem as a way to bring together and celebrate the community. Depending on what you are studying (or just plain interested in), you should ask the library about the HSCC. Other members of the HSCC are Aaron Davis Hall, the Apollo Theatre Foundation, Inc., the Boys Choir of Harlem, Inc., Dance Theatre of Harlem, the Harlem School of the Arts, Inc., Jazzmobile, Inc., the National Black Theatre, Inc., and the Studio Museum in Harlem.

The Schomburg also has exhibits, another great place to get ideas and to do research. Though there is enough text to get through the exhibit without a guide, tours are available with a reservation. They're generally given to school groups during the school day, but if you can get a group of about fifteen to twenty people together on a Saturday, the library will probably be able to accommodate you. Call (212) 491-2207 about scheduling a tour. Many past exhibits have had works published on them that are available in the museum gift shop or online.

At the library, you can learn about Arthur A. Schomburg, but you should also note the library's special tribute to Langston Hughes. As you walk past the theater named for him, look down at the floor. Above his buried ashes is a cosmogram that depicts the lifelines of Schomburg and Hughes, including their intersection in Harlem. You should definitely stop and pay your respects to the great writer this celebrates.

One important note: although the exhibits are open whenever the library is, not all divisions are open all of the time. You should go online or call to make sure that what you want to see will be available during your visit.

Notes:

South Street Seaport Museum

Address:	207 Front St. New York, NY 10038
Telephone:	212.748.8600
Directions:	Take the 2, 3, 4, 5, J, Z, or M to Fulton St. or the A or C to Broadway-Nassau. Walk east on Fulton St. to Water St.
Hours:	October-March Daily 10:00am-5:00pm Closed Mondays April-September Daily 10:00am-6:00pm Closed Mondays
Entry Fee:	$5 Adults (no student rate)
Website:	www.southstseaport.org

If you are tired of being indoors and still need to do some research, go to the South Street Seaport Museum. Although refurbished to accommodate tourists, this historic district contains a lot of information about shipping in New York before the advent of steam-powered vessels. **The museum maintains several ships, three of which are open to the public on a daily basis, as well as galleries, a library, gift shops, and administrative offices.**

Several tours run every day, leading you around the ships and the surrounding historic district. The *Ambrose*, a lighthouse ship, guided other ships into the harbor. The *Pioneer*, *Peking*, and *Wavertree*, unlike the *Ambrose*, are exclusively sail-powered. There is a tugboat, the *W.O. Decker*, and also among the working vessels is the *Lettie G. Howard*.

While the interiors of the ships are interesting by themselves, there are also fascinating exhibits on board. If you visit the *Peking*, you will learn about how its overall structure related to its function, which for many years was transporting nitrates from Chile to Europe. But when you walk on board you will also see breathtaking video shot from the top of the mast by a sailor, during a commercial voyage from Germany to Chile. While it includes shots of sea and sky that you would probably expect, it also contains footage of the men on deck performing their daily tasks.

In comparison to the *Peking*, the *Wavertree* is an older, more beautiful ship made in Britain. It once served as a school. Imagine going to school on a ship. Pretty different, huh? While this vessel is still capable of sailing, it does not go out and is currently under construction. Before you leave the docks, take a look in the model shop on the pier. It has models of several kinds of ships in exquisite detail.

During the period the Seaport is restored to, ships such as these lined the docks up and down the street, which was therefore known as "The Street of Mast." Though not all of the ships are available to visit year-round, you can rest assured that no matter what time of year you go, you will at least be able to see the *Peking* and the *Wavertree*. If you're adventurous enough and you have a little extra cash, you might want to consider being not just a visitor, but a passenger. For an addition $25, you can take a nighttime sail on the *Pioneer* (a ship built in 1885) in New York Harbor.

Okay, so maybe you're thinking this place sounds like it's really for tourists. Well, it is. But it's also for students. In fact, the South Street Seaport Museum is one of five partnered with the New York City Museum School, and it offers many educational programs you should consider. Tours for school groups include sail raises and knot tying on board the *Peking*. If you are interested in learning these skills, call and ask if you can join a school group. The majority of other educational programs are aimed at younger kids, but could be valuable in researching a variety of topics. In addition, **the organization offers internships to high school students.**

The museum galleries house a variety of exhibits on New York history, including one on the history of ocean liners, with many intricate models and even old advertisements for voyages aboard these ships. Obviously, back in the Pilgrims' day, people didn't have much choice but to endure a long, arduous journey aboard a sail-powered vessel. We all remember that part. But think ahead even past World War II. Even after industrialism and huge advances in technology, people didn't travel across continents in planes yet. The U.S. used planes to bomb and to transport military supplies, but the travel industry was still years away from carrying people across continents in airplanes.

This exhibit documents the change in trans-Atlantic boat trips from difficult, joyless journeys to pleasurable, if lengthy, outings. Perhaps the highlight is a strikingly large and accurate model of the Cunard line's *Queen Mary*, a passenger ship from the 1930s. The famed *Queen Elizabeth II* is also the subject of a part of this exhibit. While no such ships have docked at South Street Seaport since the late 19th century, they are fascinating and certainly prominent in maritime history.

Another new permanent exhibit is "All Available Boats: Harbor Voices and Images." You may not immediately think of the South Street Seaport when you think of September 11th, but on a day when bridges and tunnels were closed, ships, especially small ones manned with volunteers, played a huge role in the effort to evacuate victims from the World Trade Center in the hours following the attack. This exhibit is a small collection of audio files of New Yorkers who used boats on September 11th to help relieve the disaster in lower Manhattan and evacuate residents.

Remember that the South Street Seaport is not just about ships. It also includes the immediate neighborhood, and you'd be surprised by the history you can find here in addition to the maritime story. Bowne and Co. is a fully restored print shop where visitors can learn about printing. Another important feature of the area is the Fulton Fish Market, which, after many years of service is moving to the Bronx. Although not part of the museum, it is a famous and very busy spot that has been an integral part of the area for hundreds of years.

Most useful for research is the Melville Library, located at 213 Water Street. It contains over 20,000 volumes and is an excellent resource for anything relating to life around the New York port: **the architecture of ships, the history of Lower Manhattan, local business history, naval history, the maritime impact on westward expansion, and the Industrial Revolution's impact on shipping.** They even have some stuff you might not think to name—like a complete history of yachting, for example. Because most of this library's materials have been acquired from donated personal collections, the contents often reflect the donors' interests.

In addition to books, the library also contains many "clipping files," among which are old ship plans, business records, and the like. But while the Melville Library is a comprehensive resource in many areas of maritime history, it has some large gaps. The museum covers the turn of the century very well, but the library is specifically dedicated to maritime history and the story of the neighborhood. (So, for example, this would not be the best place to come and study immigration. Go to Ellis Island for that.) Norman Brouwer, the librarian, is available to help students with research. It is best, though, due to the library's hours, to call before visiting to ensure that it will be open: (212) 748-8648.

South Street Seaport is undergoing a great amount of construction. In 2003, a new children's gallery will open, and in 2004, an exhibit known as World Port will be complete. It will explore New York City's history and current status as an international port of commerce attracting people from all over the world. The history of the Dutch in America, trans-Atlantic slavery, and Chinese Americans will all be key components of World Port.

You should note that the South Street Seaport Museum was largely responsible for preserving the historical neighborhood in which it is located. Years ago, renovating the district with entirely modern buildings was proposed, but the museum led an effort to "save" the neighborhood. As a result, most of the old buildings are still intact. Though upcoming modern development projects are underway, the history of the area is no longer at risk of being lost, due in large part to the museum's efforts to become part of an official historic district. This spirit of preservation is prevalent in many parts of New York City, but perhaps nowhere is it stronger than at South Street Seaport. People took time out of their lives to preserve this site for future generations, like yours. You should reward their efforts by visiting what they have been able to save for you.

Caissa Douwes, an employee of the museum, can be reached at the main telephone number. She will gladly answer your questions.

Address:	Liberty Island New York, NY 10004
Telephone:	212.363.3200
Directions:	Take the 1 or 9 to South Ferry
Hours:	Daily 9:00am-5:15pm Closed Dec. 25th
Entry Fee:	$10 for the ferry: no charge to enter the statue or museum
Website:	www.nps.gov/stli

The ferry, S.S. *Miss Liberty*, transports you across the sluggish (and sludgy) waters of New York Harbor to the emerald isle of liberty. The Statue of Liberty looms over the harbor, a gigantic green symbol of baseball, white bread, apple pie, and freedom. Walking up to the base of the statue, along brick paths between emerald lawns, you feel true patriotism swelling in your breast. This single monument represents the freedom of speech, the freedom to vote for representative government, the freedom to... wait on line?!

At the foot of the Statue of Liberty lies a veritable army of tourists waiting to ascend through her nether regions to . . . I'm not sure what. The only thing awaiting them at the top is a view of Manhattan. Admittedly, there do seem to be quite a few people willing to walk up ten flights of stairs at the pace of a wounded llama in order to see the view, but we certainly don't understand. Once you've been "liberated" from the seemingly endless lines, you have the "liberty" of wandering around the well-manicured grounds. There really is nothing like ambling through a park better groomed than a prize cocker spaniel, listening to the melodious sounds of screaming tourists. This is why, as soon as possible, you should find yourself once again on the ferry, this time moving towards another symbol of hope, though also of oppression and despair: Ellis Island.

Ellis Island, as you probably know, is the famous immigration depot where thousands upon thousands of starving, desperate people waited anxiously to find out whether they would be allowed into the United States. **The enormous building that housed all the waiting and examination rooms has been converted into a museum for your educational pleasure.** The ground floor has a number of entertaining exhibits about immigration patterns. Generally geared to children, these exhibits have fascinating flashing lights, lots of bright colors, and a modicum of educational interest. Come here last.

The second floor contains the most impressive room in the building, the Great Hall. Stepping into it is like stepping into... a really big room. But it is REALLY big! It is fascinating (and terrifying) to imagine the hall filled with thousands of people, lined up throughout, waiting, and waiting, and waiting... (If you have gone ahead and tried this at the Statue of Liberty, you know what they must have gone through.) **The exhibits on the second floor are mostly concerned with immigration: how individual people got here, what they did once they were here, and what everybody else thought of them.**

Looking at this exhibit, in the place where these things really went on and where these people really walked, is a touching experience. There are quotes from many immigrants on the wall, which should prove immensely useful to you in writing your paper. (Quote an actual immigrant and it sounds as if you did your research in a time machine–very impressive.) Also, make sure to look at all the documents they have around. You can do all kinds of good things with a primary source (like get an A, for example).

After looking through the second floor (and make sure that you do **if you're writing a paper on anything that has anything to do with immigration, western migration, the Industrial Revolution, etc.**), move on up to the third floor. There, you will see many articles belonging to individual immigrants. Most interesting among these are the clothing these people wore and some of the things they picked up on the way to America. For example, an Italian immigrant showed up with a Southeast Asian instrument that he had learned to play in a holding area in the Caribbean. While these exhibits are in many ways more exciting than the ones on the second floor, they are less useful.

On the way out, you can go through all the examination rooms. They're interesting, but only really useful to your paper if you're writing specifically on the topic of immigration. On the other hand, if you are . . . never mind. Go through these rooms! When you're done with the museum, which takes a pretty long time, you must get back on line and take the ferry to Manhattan.

On the way back, while the wind plays with your hair and the sun shines on your back (we did this in summer–if you're doing it in winter, then change the above to "while you huddle together with your friends or nearby strangers for warmth"), try to reflect on what the Statue of Liberty means to all those people who were waiting on line to climb up to the top of her. We are a nation of immigrants, with so many of us (or our forebears) coming to this country to seek freedom. And while we may not have expected (or maybe we did) to find that freedom embodied in a gigantic green woman, the lines to climb into her belly no longer seem as long and tortuous once you understand what so many of our forefathers and -mothers went through to reach her.

Notes:

Studio Museum in Harlem

Address:	144 W. 125th St. New York, NY
Telephone:	212.864.4500
Directions:	Take the 2, 3, A, B, C, D, 4, 5 or 6 to W. 125th St.
Hours:	Wednesday & Thursday 12:00pm-6:00pm
	Friday 12:00pm-8:00pm
	Saturday & Sunday 10:00am-6:00pm
	Closed Mondays & Tuesdays
Entry Fee:	$3 Students
Website:	www.studiomuseuminharlem.org

The Studio Museum in Harlem is not very large, so it does not have a great deal of helpful research topic information. However, the few exhibits that it does have, depending on what you are studying, could turn out to be very helpful to you. **Though the museum focuses on African-American art and artists of African descent and the majority of the artwork is contemporary, some of these may provide an interesting study to include in your history paper.**

Four exhibits were on display when we visited. The first, "Expanding the Walls: Making Connections between Photography, History and Community," is a series of photographs made by students in a museum-run program. The students modeled their work after hotographer James Van Der Zee (1886-1983). The students, like Van Der Zee, wandered the streets and took pictures of people and places throughout Harlem. Their photographs, which are on display alongside some of Van Der Zee's, are very powerful images. One by Jerome Greene entitled *Can't Carry Me* depicts an empty, abandoned stroller. These snapshots go beyond everyday life to capture themes that are as relevant today as 75 years ago when Van Der Zee was shooting. Accompanying the exhibit is a book on Van Der Zee's work and a notebook of comments by the student photographers.

A second exhibit explored the work of Beauford Delaney (1901-1979), one of ten kids born to a Methodist minister in Knoxville, TN. He trained as an artist at the Art Students League while participating in the bohemian scene of Harlem and Greenwich Village. Delaney spent the 1950's in Paris with James Baldwin, among others. The exhibit focuses on his use of the color yellow, which he believed to have healing and redemptive qualities. His displayed works range from the colorful to the monotone and from the realistic to the abstract and outright bizarre. The styles of his portraits are as varied as the people in them. To give you an idea, just a few of the people he paints include Stanislas Rodanski, Marion Anderson, Ahmed Bioud, James Baldwin, Howard Swanson, Bernard Hassel, Ella Fitzgerald, and himself.

Unfortunately, this exhibit, like the remaining two, "Edgar Arceneaux: Drawings of Removal" and "Ironic/Iconic," is very much based on art and not history. "Edgar Arceneaux" is an ongoing project in which the artist is painting a room in the museum. "Ironic/Iconic" is comprised of works by artists in residence. These exhibits won't really help you with general research. However, **these pieces, especially the work by Adia Millet, may be helpful if your history project is culturally oriented.** You could use the more political pieces, for example, to show how so many issues of the past are still relevant and how many struggles of the past are still unresolved in American society today.

A number of upcoming exhibits have subjects with historical importance, including "Harlem Postcards"; "Photography Past/Forward: Aperture at 50," a show that will contain hundreds of historic photographs; "Challenge of the Modern: African American Artists 1925-1945"; and "Frederick J. Brown: Portraits in Jazz, Blues, and Other Icons." For more information about the exhibits, you should check out the museum's website.

The museum runs several programs. Every week it hosts Uptown Fridays, free with museum admission, which are nights filled with the music and culture of Harlem. A large number of programs are organized for the first Saturday of each month, when admission to both the museum and programs are free. Just some of the museum's programs include lectures by artists, authors, and educators; concerts; workshops; and walking tours of Harlem. Recently the museum held eight free sessions called Words in Motion, where participants learned about creating visual arts, poetry, and how to DJ. Though the museum's programs tend to be contemporary, because they are also very cultural, you may be able to find some of the programs useful for a research paper in American history. For a list of current programs and any fees or registration deadlines, visit the website.

Though the museum has no place available for students to research, it does have an extensive gift shop. Students on a tight budget can examine book titles for suggestions on library research sources.

Whitney Museum of American Art

Address:	945 Madison Ave at E. 75th St. New York, NY 10021
Telephone:	212.570.3676
Directions:	Take the 6 to E. 77th St.
Hours:	Tuesday-Thursday 11:00am-6:00pm
	Fridays 1:00pm-9:00pm
	Saturday & Sunday 11:00am-6:00pm
	Closed Mondays
	Fridays 6:00pm-9:00pm Pay what you wish
Entry Fee:	$9.50 Students
	Students with valid NYC Public Schools ID free
Website:	www.whitney.org

The Whitney Museum has one of the best collections of 20th-century American art in the world. It includes over 12,000 works: paintings, sculptures, prints, photographs, drawings, and more. The permanent collection includes works by Edward Hopper, Alexander Calder, Louise Nevelson, Claes Oldenburg, Georgia O'Keefe, Jackson Pollock, and Mark Rothko. Though the museum is not able to display its entire collection at once, the objects on exhibit at any given time represent a complete overview of the 20th century in American art.

So if you are studying art movements, American art, or anything else in the 20th century, visit this museum! The lower-floor galleries are arranged by period, with text panels and object labels on the walls providing historical context. The top floors have rotating exhibits, usually featuring single artists. There are free daily tours of the floors and exhibits.

The Whitney offers several programs for students. Besides courting school group visits, it also offers workshops that allow high school students to discuss prominent artworks with the artists who made them. They have independent study programs as well: the Studio, Curatorial, and Critical Studies programs. Only 25 students are chosen for these, and they last an entire school year. For information, call (212) 431-1737. For a full list of current programs available to the public in general, visit the website.

The museum's Francis Mulhall Achilles Library contains the world's most comprehensive research collection in 20th-century American art. In addition to the special collections and archives, this is an invaluable resource. Although the librarians usually only work with scholars, they can answer questions and send lists of resources. You can call the library at (212) 570-3648 or e-mail at 4library@whitney.org. Be sure to leave plenty of time to receive an answer (i.e., several days). You can search the library and museum holdings through "WhitneyCat" on their website. You should also check the website for a list of current and upcoming exhibits.

Useful Websites

We figured we could save you some of the headache that we'd already gone through. There are many other types of museums out there. And the best way to find the museums is to go online. Once you've found one that specializes in your topic, you might save some time by asking a staff member to recommend other places. But to find that first place, you'll really want to use the Web.

Now, if you're wondering where you can get online, fret no longer. You should be able to use computers at your school. If you can't, go to the closest library. You may be limited in the amount of time you can spend online, and you may have to sign up earlier in the day and come back during your time slot, but don't be discouraged. The Internet is one of the best ways to do preliminary research. It can save you a lot of time and energy. If you're unsure how to use it, ask a friend, a teacher, or a librarian. People are around who can help. You just need to ask.

To find out about Gilder Lehrman and to start your research, try our website:
www.gilderlehrman.org
While we aren't a museum, we have all sorts of interesting and useful American history material on our website. After all, American history is what we do.

The library is also great place to get started finding out about museums and doing research.
www.nypl.org (Manhattan, Staten Island, and the Bronx)
www.queenslibrary.org
www.brooklynpubliclibrary.org

If you search a borough with words like "cultural institutions" or "museums" on the library's website, you can come up with some great search results, such as:
http://www2.nypl.org/home/branch/bronx/culture.cfm
http://www2.nypl.org/home/branch/staten/culture.cfm

If you're doing research on a particular community or will be going there to do research, try searching a borough and a word like "community" on the library web. When we did that for Manhattan, we found this list of useful websites: (please turn the page)

http://www2.nypl.org/home/branch/links/index3.cfm?STwoID=101

If you would rather search the entire web, we recommend using **www.google.com**

If you are looking for religious institutions, try starting here:
http://www.barnard.columbia.edu/religion/pages/nylinks.html

These were some of the more useful sites for museums we found.
http://www.ny.com/museums/all.museums.html
http://www.theinsider.com/nyc/museums/museums.htm
http://www.readio.com/museums/nycmuseums.html

To check out bus and subway maps, go to:
http://www.mta.nyc.ny.us/mta/maps.htm

And whatever you do, don't forget about High 5!
http://www.high5tix.org/
We suggest making High 5 your new best friend. Okay, that's a slight exaggeration... But seriously, people are making things cheap and accessible to you. Go take advantage of this while you still can. Pretty soon you'll be too old and it won't be any easier to find or afford good tickets. Trust us, we know.

A few more helpful websites about New York City and history and the arts:
http://www.nyc.gov/html/culture/html/culture.html
http://newyork.citysearch.com/
http://www.nyc-arts.org/nyc-arts/master_parent.html
http://www.forgotten-ny.com/
http://www.nytimes.com/pages/nytoday/
http://www.nycvisit.com/home/index.cfm
http://www.timeoutny.com/

So what are you waiting for? Go get started!

 Layout & Design by Design for Good. Illustrations by Francis Floro, Jason Heuer, Youngsun Lee, and Yael Daphna Saar.

Notes:

Notes:

Notes:

Notes:

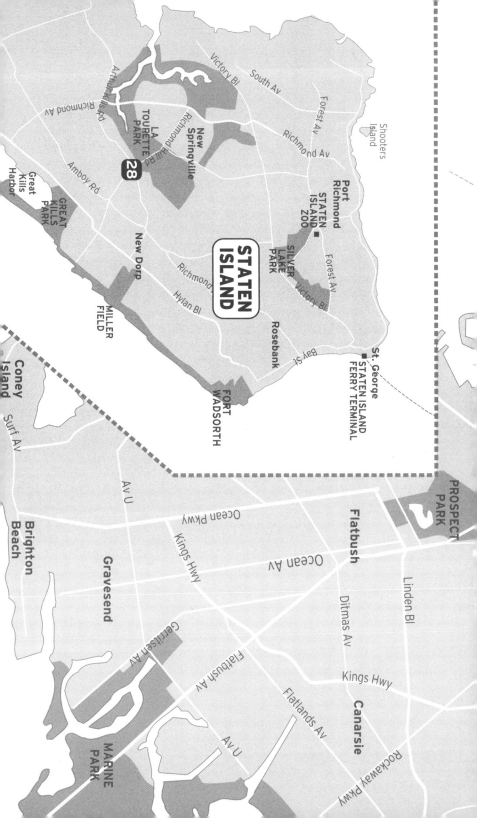

QUEENS

25 American Museum of the Moving Image

26 Museum of Modern Art QNS

BROOKLYN

27 Brooklyn Museum of Art

STATEN ISLAND

28 Historic Richmond Town

MANHATTAN

16 American Folk Art Museum
9 American Museum of Natural History
14 Americas Society
8 Cooper-Hewitt, National Design Museum (Smithsonian)
13 Frick Collection
2 Hamilton Grange
15 Intrepid Sea-Air-Space Museum
7 Jewish Museum
19 Lower East Side Tenement Museum
11 Metropolitan Museum of Art
1 Morris-Jumel Mansion
6 Museo del Barrio
21 Museum of American Financial History
20 Museum of Chinese in the Americas
5 Museum of the City of New York
17 Museum of Television and Radio
22 National Museum of the American Indian (Smithsonian)
10 New-York Historical Society
18 New York Public Library
3 Schomburg Center for Research in Black Culture
23 South Street Seaport Museum
24 Statue of Liberty and Ellis Island
4 Studio Museum in Harlem
12 Whitney Museum of American Art

Mission Statement

The Gilder Lehrman Institute of American History promotes the study and love of American history. We organize seminars and enrichment programs for teachers and National Park Service educators; create history-centered high schools nationwide; support and produce publications and traveling exhibitions for students and the general public; sponsor lectures by historians; develop electronic media projects, including the Institute's website; establish research centers at universities and libraries; and grant and oversee fellowships for scholars to work in the Gilder Lehrman Collection and in other archives of American history.